Business Studies

David Floyd

Stephen Wood

Contents

Examination boards	3
AS exams	4
Successful revision	5
How to boost your grade	6

Chapter 1

The external environment	7
Questions with model answers	7
Exam practice questions	11
Exam practice answers	12

Chapter 2

Business organisations	14
Questions with model answers	14
Exam practice questions	18
Exam practice answers	20

Chapter 3

Structure and growth	22
Questions with model answers	22
Exam practice questions	26
Exam practice answers	28

Chapter 4

External influences	32
Questions with model answers	32
Exam practice questions	36
Exam practice answers	39

Chapter 5

Accounting and finance	44
Questions with model answers	44
Exam practice questions	48
Exam practice answers	51

Chapter 6

Human resources management	55
Questions with model answers	55
Exam practice questions	59
Exam practice answers	61

Chapter 7

Marketing	65
Questions with model answers	65
Exam practice questions	69
Exam practice answers	71

Chapter 8

Productive efficiency	74
Questions with model answers	74
Exam practice questions	76
Exam practice answers	78

Mock Exams

Mock Exam 1	
Objectives and External Environment	81
Mock Exam 2	
HRM and Operations Management	84
Mock Exam 3	
Accounting & Finance and Marketing	87

Mock Exam Answers

Mock Exam 1	
Objectives and External Environment	90
Mock Exam 2	
HRM and Operations Management	92
Mock Exam 3	
Accounting & Finance and Marketing	94

Examination boards

AQA Assessment and Qualifications Alliance
Devas Street,
Manchester,
M15 6EX
www.aqa.org.uk

EDEXCEL
Stewart House,
32 Russell Square,
London,
WC1B 5DN
www.edexcel.org.uk

OCR Oxford Cambridge and RSA Examinations
1 Hills Road,
Cambridge,
CB1 2EU
www.ocr.org.uk

CCEA Northern Ireland Council for Curriculum, Examinations and Assessment
29 Clarendon Road,
Belfast,
BT1 3BG
www.ccea.org.uk

WJEC Welsh Joint Education Committee
245 Western Avenue,
Cardiff,
CF5 2YX
www.wjec.co.uk

AQA
The three AS Units are tested by stimulus response questions (Unit 1) and questions based on a pre-release case study (common to Units 2 and 3).

Edexcel
The AS Units are tested by questions on a pre-issue case study common to all three Units.

OCR
At AS level, Unit 1 is tested by questions on a pre-seen case study, Unit 2 by a data response paper, and Unit 3 by questions based on a pre-issued case study.

CCEA
Each of three AS Units has its own written paper.

WJEC
At AS level, all Units consist of stimulus–response questions, and there are also some short-answer questions in Unit 1.

AS exams

Different types of questions

Structured questions

In A level Business Studies exams, unit tests often use structured questions requiring both short answers and more extended answers. These questions are often in several parts, each of which may be further subdivided. They may be linked directly to data on a given context in the form of a paragraph or short article about a real or imagined business situation. This introductory data provides the major part of the information to be used, and indicates clearly what the question is about.

Structured questions are popular at AS level. The parts to these questions become progressively more demanding as you work your way through them.

Extended answers

Business Studies questions requiring more extended answers may form part of structured questions, or may form separate questions. These may also be linked to a 'scenario' or case study, and are often used to assess your ability to communicate ideas and to assemble a logical argument.

The 'correct' answers to extended questions are often less well-defined than those requiring shorter answers.

What examiners look for

- Examiners are obviously looking for correct points, although these may not match the wording in the examiner's marking scheme exactly.
- Your answer will score high marks if it contains accurate content and shows that you can apply, analyse and evaluate this content in the context of the question. You will not receive extra marks for writing a lot of words or through simply repeating information.
- Examiners expect you to reach a logical conclusion based on the arguments presented in your answer.

What makes an A, C and E grade candidate?

Obviously, you want to get the highest grade you possibly can. The way to do this is to make sure you have a good all-round knowledge and understanding of Business Studies.

- **A grade candidates** have a wide knowledge of Business Studies and can apply that knowledge to new situations. They are equally strong in all of the modules. A likely minimum mark for an A grade candidate is 75%.
- **C grade candidates** have a reasonable knowledge of Business Studies, but they are less effective when applying their knowledge to new situations. They may also have weaknesses in some of the modules. A likely minimum mark for a C grade candidate is 50%.
- **E grade candidates** have a limited knowledge of Business Studies, and have not learnt how to apply their ideas effectively to new situations. They find it harder to express their knowledge, and fail to give full answers. A likely minimum mark for an E grade is 40%.

Successful revision

Revision skills

- Develop a 'revision routine', e.g. by doing revision in the same place and about the same time each day.
- Prepare a revision plan for a topic, e.g. review next day, then re-read two weeks later.
- Start with a topic with which you are familiar.
- Re-read topics, to reinforce your learning.
- If you make revision notes, identify key points such as the main business theme or issue.
- Vary the style of your notes, e.g. by producing 'spider diagrams', patterned notes or mnemonics.
- Limit the time you spend (e.g. 30 to 40 minutes) before taking a break.
- Stop before you get too tired.
- Leave something easy with which to start your revision the next day.
- Don't stay up late the night before an exam trying to learn new topics. You will have forgotten much of it by the morning, and the lack of sleep may affect your performance in the exam.

Practice questions

This book is designed to help you get better results.

- Study the grade A and C candidates' answers, and see if you could have done better.
- Try the exam practice questions, and then check the answers.
- Make sure you understand why the answers given are correct.
- When you feel ready, try the AS mock exam papers.

If you perform well on the questions in this book, you should do well in the examination.

Planning and timing your answers in the exam

- You should spend the first few minutes of the assessment reading through the whole question paper.
- When answering structured questions, do not feel that you have to complete one part before starting the next. The further you are into a question, the more difficult the marks can be to obtain. If you run out of ideas, go on to the next part/question.
- You need to respond to as many parts of questions as possible. You will not score well if you spend so long trying to perfect the first questions that you do not reach later questions at all.
- Use the mark allocation to guide you on how much to write, and on how many different points to make.
- Plan your answers: don't write down the first thing that comes into your head.
- Make sure your plan reminds you to refer to any relevant information in the given case study/situation.
- Make sure you give a balanced answer where required.
- Allow some time at the end to read through your answers.

How to boost your grade

Organisation
- Organise your main and revision notes carefully, keeping them in a file.
- If you use highlighter pens or underlining to emphasise sections of your notes, make sure you limit their use to the really important points.

Research
- Spend some time reading the 'broadsheet' newspapers or other sources of up-to-date business information.
- Make brief summaries of business developments: you may be able to mention these developments when answering the exam questions.
- This research will also help you with coursework projects.

Answering the question
- Make sure you read and study the data before you tackle the questions.
- You'll rarely find that a question is one-sided in outcome, so always give a balanced answer/conclusion.
- Keep referring back to the question for information you may need to extract or comment on in your answer.
- If you decide to start by answering the question you think you can do best first, don't spend over-long on this question because you will lose valuable time needed to construct answers to the other questions.

Words and figures
- Marks are not only given for correct spelling, punctuation and grammar: you'll score higher marks if you can use business terms and language suitably.
- Study and become familiar with the key terms used in the main functional areas: marketing, accounting, human resource management and production.
- Be particularly careful when using accounting terms: for example, profit and cash are different, and so are profit and profitability.
- You should make sure that your answer is clear, easy to read and concise.
- If possible, estimate any numerical answer first.
- Check any calculations you have made, and make sure that your answer is sensible. Is it given in the correct units (e.g. £000)? Does it look right? Show all you workings.

Diagrams and formulae
- Check whether you will be given formulae in the exam, e.g. for standard deviation or time series calculations. If so, you don't need to waste time memorising them, BUT you still need to understand how the formula is constructed, why it exists and what it calculates.
- You should make sure that any graphs, charts or other diagrams are correctly labelled, given a relevant heading, and have a suitable scale that fills (most of) the graph paper.

Chapter 1 — The external environment

Questions with model answers

NICDR Ltd plans to export

NICDR Ltd is a manufacturer of CD ROMs. It took part in an IDB trade mission 18 months ago and, as a result, is now exporting to the Middle East. Sales are good but there are many problems involved in transporting goods from Northern Ireland to the Middle East. For this reason NICDR Ltd is considering setting up a manufacturing base in Dubai, in the Middle East.

NICDR Ltd is currently involved in discussions with Acorba, a small manufacturer of CD ROMs already established in Dubai. Acorba would favour a joint venture arrangement but NICDR Ltd would prefer to either establish its own new factory and manufacture the CD ROMs in Dubai or take over Acorba as an overseas subsidiary and carry out the manufacturing there.

Examiner's Commentary

For help see Revise AS Study Guide pp. 26–29, 32–40, 52–58.

(a) Outline the meaning of the following terms:

  (i) 'multinational' [2]

  (ii) 'joint venture' [2]

  (iii) 'trade mission' [2]

  (iv) 'subsidiary'. [2]

(b) (i) Explain how IDB trade missions can benefit such firms as NICDR Ltd. [6]

  'IDB' refers to Industrial Development Board.

  (ii) Suggest reasons why NICDR Ltd might decide to expand its international operations by manufacturing in its own factory in Dubai rather than agreeing to a joint venture with Acorba. [4]

(c) Evaluate the impact on Dubai of NICDR Ltd deciding to set up its own new factory in that country. [12]

[CCEA, 2000]

C grade candidate – mark scored 15/30

Examiner's Commentary

(a) (i) This is a firm with branches in another country.

(ii) Firms agree to work together to make profits, but they also have to share costs.

(iii) A government body goes abroad in an attempt to win trade for its economy.

(iv) A firm that is owned by another firm.

Although only worth 2 marks each, these are limited descriptions, and (i) is an incomplete definition of a multinational.

(b) (i) A trade mission will organise matters for a company such as NICDR Ltd. As a result, the company finds it a lot easier to deal with overseas organisations, because it can rely on the trade mission to establish links.

(ii) The benefit to NICDR Ltd is that it will remain in full control of the work. Its own managers can take all the decisions, and work exclusively for the benefit of NICDR Ltd.

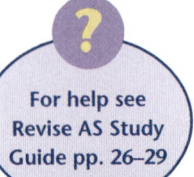

For help see Revise AS Study Guide pp. 26–29

The answer to part (ii) is rather brief, and – although it contains key phrases such as 'full control' and 'work exclusively' – one point only is being made.

(c) Dubai will gain through having an additional firm in its economy, which will be bringing in advanced technology and working arrangements. This will stimulate the economy, and help develop this CD ROM industry, which will in time lead to exports. The problems that Dubai will face include a possible increase in home-based employment, and the fact that NICDR Ltd can withdraw from the country when it likes. Since NICDR Ltd is in control of its own affairs, it can also 'export' its profits, if it gains financially by doing so (e.g. through a better tax regime in the UK). Some multinationals have exploited overseas economies and created pollution, and NICDR could possibly do this, which would again disadvantage Dubai.

It is likely that Dubai can survive without NICDR, especially since it is an oil-rich country, and it may be better not to let too many multinationals dominate its economy.

There are some strong arguments presented against NICDR, though these are not fully developed, and some important arguments in favour of its presence in Dubai are ignored. A more balanced answer should have been presented.

GRADE BOOSTER

To score more marks, you normally either have to include more points, or expand fully the single point being made.

A grade candidate – mark scored 29/30

Examiner's Commentary

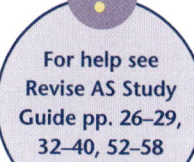

For help see Revise AS Study Guide pp. 26–29, 32–40, 52–58

(a) (i) A multinational is a business with its headquarters in one country, but with manufacturing or assembly plants in at least one other.

(ii) A joint venture takes place when (at least) two firms set up a division that will be operated jointly by them. They share the costs and responsibilities, and also any profits, from the joint venture.

Brief but precise answers are needed for both marks.

(iii) A trade mission takes place to another country, having been organised by a government department or other official body (e.g. IDB), in an attempt to boost trade through showing what that country's firms can provide.

(iv) A subsidiary is a company that, whilst normally trading under its own name, is owned by another (the holding company) through share ownership (normally 50+% of the voting shares).

(b) (i) NICDR has some experience of the value of trade missions: 'as a result, it is now exporting...'. The main benefit of trade missions to NICDR is one of providing expertise and support, particularly in new markets where the company has no experience. The missions give companies like NICDR the opportunity to meet potential clients, agents or distributors, as well as to undertake some market research. Because the missions tend to organise these trips, dealing with all the administration, this proves a cost-effective way for the company to explore whether it is worthwhile exporting to, or expanding in, the market.

This candidate has related the answer to key business functions, such as administration, marketing and finance.

(ii) By having their own factory, NICDR will be in full control of the operation. If they were in a joint venture with Acorba, the responsibility for the operation would have to be shared: as a result, decisions could take longer to make and to implement, potentially leading to a loss of competitiveness.

Part (ii) of the question asks for 'reasons', so at least two reasons explained in some detail – as here – are required.

Furthermore, in the joint venture the firms would share the profits: if NICDR retains control, it keeps all profits itself. These profits might well be higher due to the quicker decision-making, although NICDR may at first lack direct local contact with the market, compared with working more closely with Acorba, and this might reduce profits to start with.

The external environment

A grade continued

(c) The benefits to Dubai are likely to include a higher level of gross national product as a result of more employment. The standard of living will therefore rise. The fact that more CD ROMs are likely to be produced may lead to exports from Dubai, which would improve its balance of payments through more exports (also possibly fewer imports, if production increases and can satisfy home demand for CD ROMs). Having a new factory in Dubai should bring new, efficient work practices into the country, and create additional competition for local firms: this should improve efficiency overall, thereby making the country's economy that much more competitive.

However, as a multinational with its headquarters overseas, NICDR is in a position to act in its own interests rather than those of Dubai. One example here is that NICDR may decide to move its profits out of Dubai if it can save tax by doing so. A second cause for concern will arise if there is damage to the local environment, e.g. from the manufacturing process. Also, it is likely that the local competition stimulated by NICDR will lead to closures of some Dubai-based firms, possibly creating high local unemployment.

On balance, I think that NICDR's presence in Dubai is likely to prove beneficial, especially since it is a 'high-tech' company bringing up-to-date technological expertise into the country, which will have a 'knock-on' effect.

Examiner's Commentary

The question asks for an evaluation, and this candidate is providing a well-balanced evaluative answer that looks at both sides of the argument.

A well-structured and properly explained answer that relates the general issues of a multinational presence to the specific situation given in the question.

Exam practice questions

Read the following passage and then answer the question that follows.

1 Business failures in Wales in 1999 increased by 26% when compared with the previous year. Late payment, according to Dun and Bradstreet's business information survey, is a major factor and the worst-hit victims are likely to be the small firms.

Source: adapted from The *Western Mail*, 5 January 2000

Discuss the view that there is no future for small businesses in the United Kingdom economy. [11]

[WJEC, 2000]

---

2 The figures below show male and female employment (full-time, part-time and self-employed) in the UK 1985–2000 (figures in millions).

Table 1

	1985	1990	1995	2000
Males	14.2	15.2	14.3	15.4
Females	10.1	11.6	11.6	12.3
Total	24.3	26.8	25.9	27.7

Source: *Employment in Europe 1998–2000* (European Commission)

(a) Explain the term *self-employed*. [2]

(b) Consider the factors that might have led to the trends shown in **Table 1**. [5]

Peninsula Ltd is a small construction business. Demand for its services has fluctuated, but recently it has won a big contract to convert an old factory into flats. This will last for only nine months and the directors of the business intend to take on extra full-time workers. However, there is a risk that at the end of the nine-month period some of these workers will lose their jobs.

Source: adapted from 'Part-time workers must be treated same as full-timers': *The Sunday Times,* 20 May 2001

Using **Table 1** and the extract above, answer the following questions.

(c) Evaluate the possible effects of changing trends in employment on construction firms like Peninsula Ltd. [10]

(d) Analyse how fluctuations in demand might affect Peninsula Ltd. [9]

[Edexcel, January 2003]

Answers

(1) *Knowledge*

- The limitations of small firms include: difficulty in raising finance, lack of specialist expertise, few if any economies of scale. However, small firms remain the most popular size of business organisation in the UK economy. **(1–3 marks)**

Application/Understanding

There are several reasons why small firms continue to survive.

- Their willingness to provide products that larger firms don't wish to supply: examples include supplying components for a large firm, or a specialist service such as providing foodstuffs or cleaning services.
- They may operate in a specific niche or specialist market with local/limited demand: examples include 'collector' firms (e.g. stamp and model collecting), and local shops such as hairdressers or specialist foodstuffs.
- They may provide a particular skill that is best suited to small-scale operation or subject to limited demand (e.g. local accountants and estate agents).
- Simply as a result of being small, these firms are often better able to adapt quickly to changing market conditions. **(4–8 marks)**

Analysis

- We can assume the following conditions will continue to exist in the UK economy – the need for specialists, and the existence of small-scale or local demand.
- As a result, there is no reason why small firms cannot continue to survive. **(9–11 marks)**

> **examiner's tip** To gain most of the 11 marks available, you should give specific examples of situations where small firms continue to thrive.

---

(2) (a) *Knowledge*

- A person is working as his or her own boss.
- For example, many electricians, plumbers and other tradespeople are self-employed because they work for themselves. **(1–2 marks)**

(b) *Knowledge*

- Trends seen in Table 1 are increasing female employment, fluctuating male employment, and increasing total employment. **(1–2 marks)**

Application/Understanding

- Factors include the changing economic climate in the UK, and the changing structure of UK industry.
- More people now work in the tertiary sector, and employment in the primary and secondary sectors has fallen.
- Women often have an appropriate range of skills for tertiary work.
- Women are often more flexible, which again often suits employers in the tertiary sector. **(3–5 marks)**

(c) *Knowledge*
- One trend is the increase in the number of part-time workers.
- Another trend is the increase in the number of women available for work.

(1–2 marks)

Application/Understanding
- Peninsula Ltd could make use of part-time workers, because the extra work is likely to be for a limited time period only.
- Traditionally, male workers are more likely to have the construction skills required by Peninsula, so the additional women workers may be less relevant in this context.

(3–4 marks)

Analysis
- With part-time and women workers, there is likely to be greater flexibility for Peninsula when recruiting and retaining staff.
- The business will find it easier to recruit and get rid of part-time staff.
- Costs may also be lower, because part-time staff may be prepared to receive a lower rate of pay.

(5–6 marks)

Evaluation
- The rise in overall employment numbers may not be that relevant to a construction firm, because of the increase in women workers.
- If part-time staff are to be employed, they may lack loyalty to the firm, which can result in an increase in its costs.
- This increase results from the need for extra supervision, also higher wastage levels, more frequent absences and a lower quality output.

(7–10 marks)

> **examiner's tip**
> The key to a good answer here is in recognising typical employment in the construction industry.

(d) *Knowledge*
- Changing demand will affect Peninsula's demand for factors of production.
- Demand changes due to a variety of factors, such as changes in tastes and fashion, and the introduction of new technology.

(1–3 marks)

Application/Understanding
- In the case of Peninsula, changes in demand may affect its cost structure, for example increased costs due to employing more staff (or laying staff off).
- If demand increases, the company should have increased income: a fall in demand will decrease its income.

(4–6 marks)

Analysis
- Peninsula should consider how fluctuations in demand can be coped with.
- For example, the company may decide to (or have to) promote its new buildings to a greater extent.
- It also needs to review its cost structure in order to cope with increases and decreases in the demand for its properties.

(7–9 marks)

> **examiner's tip**
> Your answer should reflect the fact that 'fluctuations' in demand refers to both increases and decreases.

Chapter 2

Business organisations

Questions with model answers

Virgin Group goes public

After the flotation in 1987, Richard Branson held 55% of the Virgin Group; the outside investors held 34%. Each share had been sold at 140 pence so that Virgin Group plc was valued at £240 million.

Most people think that 50% of a public company is the key to controlling it. While this is true in theory, to a large extent control is lost just by having to appoint non-executive directors and generally giving up time to satisfy the City. During the year that flotation took place, Virgin was arguably less creative than ever. At least 50% of the time was spent heading off to the City to explain what the company was doing to fund managers, financial advisers and City PR firms, rather than just getting on and doing it.

Richard Branson was reluctant to follow British tradition and pay out a large dividend. He preferred the American or Japanese tradition whereby a company concentrates on reinvesting its profits to build itself and increase share value.

Source: adapted from *Losing my Virginity: The Autobiography* by Richard Branson (Virgin Publishing, 2000)

(a) Briefly explain how a public limited company differs from a private limited company. [4]

(b) Discuss how Virgin's stakeholders may be affected by the switch to becoming a public limited company. [10]

(c) In 1988, Richard Branson decided to change the company back to a private limited company, with the financial help of Japanese investors. Discuss the benefits to be gained from this decision. [15]

Examiner's Commentary

? For help see Revise AS Study Guide pp. 34–38

C grade candidate – mark scored 14/29

(a) Public limited companies can sell their shares to the public and will be found on the Stock Exchange. They must have £50 000-worth of shares. Private limited companies are usually family-owned and family-run.

Examiner's Commentary: Some basic knowledge but not very clearly expressed. It is a *minimum* of £50 000 of shares.

(b) Stakeholders include shareholders, employees, suppliers, customers and the community. The community is a stakeholder because the company will create jobs in the area and provide business for other local firms. However, a company can also create problems because of pollution. By becoming a public limited company, Virgin will probably get bigger, which may provide more jobs but will also cause more pollution.

Employees may gain better job security, but will now be part of a bigger organisation and so become more of a 'name and number', whereas before they felt more a part of the company.

The new shareholders will benefit from the flotation, because they will now get a share of Virgin's profits although Richard Branson will get to keep less. The suppliers may now feel safer dealing with a bigger more financially sound company. The customers may benefit from lower prices.

Examiner's Commentary: Good start by clearly showing who stakeholders are.

If the answer had made better use of the evidence in the case study and evaluated the issues it would have gained more marks.

(c) Turning the company back into a private limited company means that Richard Branson will not have to give any profits to shareholders. He will be able to reinvest profits into new ideas for the future, which will be good for the company.

He will be able to make decisions without having to explain them to people in the city, and the time he has been spending doing this can be spent more profitably. Virgin will also be able to ensure that they do not lose control of the company and can keep more financial information secret, as company reports do not have to be made public.

Examiner's Commentary: 'Discuss' means that the examiners want you to present a reasoned argument, examining different points of view. You need to use the context and for top marks come to a reasoned decision. See page 13 of Revise AS Business Studies for more detail about what different words used by examiners mean.

GRADE BOOSTER: To score more marks always make full use of the context.

A grade candidate – mark scored 27/29

Examiner's Commentary

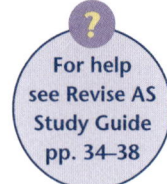

For help see Revise AS Study Guide pp. 34–38

(a) A public limited company is able to advertise and sell its shares to the public, whereas a private limited company can only sell its shares privately to friends and family. Also, shares of private limited companies can only be transferred or sold with the other shareholders' permission. The public limited company's shares may be quoted on the Stock Market, with a minimum share capital of £50 000.

(b) One group of stakeholders greatly affected by the change are the owners. The main owner before flotation was Richard Branson himself, along with a number of friends and family. During this time the profits made were reinvested and not distributed to the owners. Now as a public limited company, some of its profits will have to be distributed to the shareholders to ensure that they are kept happy and remain as shareholders. If the shareholders are not satisfied with the size of the dividend, they may sell their shares, so reducing the price of the shares and hence the value of the company.
Alternatively, they may take their complaints to the AGM, leading to bad publicity.

Clear reaction by the shareholders is analysis, which is awarded with more than half marks.

As well as dividends the flotation of the company causes a divorce between ownership and control. Although Richard Branson is still the majority shareholder, he has to bear in mind other shareholders when decisions are made. The fact that he had to spend 50% of his time visiting these other shareholders is evidence that they have to be kept informed.

This paragraph shows good links between theory and the use of evidence from the case study.

The banks, as a stakeholder, may benefit from the decision to float the company. As the company will now have greater equity as a source of capital, the debt provided by the bank will make up a smaller and less risky proportion of Virgin's finance.

Customers may find that they are now being less well served by the public limited company. As Richard Branson declares himself, the year after flotation saw less creativity taking place, which is what Virgin are famous for. If less time is being spent on new ideas then arguably the customers will not be getting a constant supply of new and better products.

To gain 9 or 10 marks this candidate's answer would need to show the potential conflict that exists in trying to satisfy different shareholders.

(c) Whilst it is a public limited company with shareholders, a business like Virgin is at the mercy of the City and must do everything to keep the City happy. The distribution of dividends is expected and, as stated in the article, is relatively high in the UK. This money may be better reinvested into a growing company such as Virgin. By returning to being a private limited company Virgin can concentrate again on the most important aspect of running a business – namely, producing new products of a high quality.

A grade continued

Examiner's Commentary

Another problem of being a public limited company is that factors outside the company's control can have a major effect. Lack of confidence in the stock market may lead to a large fall in share prices of all companies. In this case, the value of Virgin will fall by many millions of pounds. This will have serious effects on the financing of the firm, if it has debt secured against the company's balance sheet. If the company is now worth less because of a stock market crash, it may be forced to cut its borrowing or find that the banks, to compensate for the higher risk, increase the cost of borrowing.

The City is mainly interested in the short-term performance of a company. For a company such as Virgin involved in many different industries - many at their early stage of development such as the airline, mobile phones and finance - the short-term returns may be poor. This may reduce the attractiveness of Virgin shares and so push down their value.

> The candidate makes a clearly evaluative comment to guarantee high marks.

I assume that when Richard Branson made the decision to buy back the shares he took these factors into account. Although the extra finance available from being a public limited company is helpful, it may well have been at the expense of having to pander to the fund managers and financial advisers, seeing profits leaking out of the company and accepting that the public success of the company is affected by factors outside its control or influence.

> A common way to answer a question about the benefits of making a decision is to outline the problems with the alternative, or of not making that decision.

Exam practice questions

THE DOT.COMILLIONAIRE

'£440 000. Is that all?'

It was the final humiliation. Only nine months earlier Rupert's business *vitahealth.com* had floated onto the stock market in a wave of publicity and champagne. Newspapers trumpeted 'the latest dot.comillionaire' as Rupert's 20% stake received a stock market value of £12 million. Now the liquidator was only able to raise £440 000 for all the assets of the business. Suppliers, staff and the banks would not be impressed, as *vitahealth.com* had debts of over £27 million.

Rupert could not understand what went wrong. The business had started so brightly. His brainwave (well, it was a friend's really) had been to create a web site 'for those who care about their body'. Friends, helpers and City contacts had raised most of the early finance. This enabled him to buy in the programming expertise needed to create a very slick web site. As he had argued: 'if it's about looking good, it's got to look good'.

The site was to contain a listing of every health club and gym in Britain, complete with details of facilities, equipment, opening hours, membership fees and much else. There were also to be sections on Healthy Food and Living, Eating Out and Eating In. The idea was to charge for a listing on the site and to charge for advertising space for those aiming at young, fit high-spenders. It proved harder to achieve than expected, but in three months *vitahealth.com* went live in a blaze of publicity. Rupert spent £150 000 (a fifth of his start-up capital) on public relations, so it was no surprise to see his face and name all over the papers and local TV news programmes.

The early days were wonderful. The publicity led to a surge of interest by the public and the industry itself. Nearly 100 extra clubs signed up with Rupert in the three weeks after launch. Things continued to spiral upwards as the media kept Rupert's profile high, thanks in part to his social life. Photos of Rupert's £75 000 company sports car appeared regularly.

Within 6 months the business was outstripping its offices and finances. A merchant banker suggested a stock market listing and within five weeks the offer documents were prepared. The offer went superbly, raising more than £50 million for developing the business, plus £6 million for Rupert.

Immediately *vitahealth.com* plc bought a £5 million ten-year lease on beautiful offices on London's Park Lane. He was convinced that hiring top people meant having the very best working conditions. He joked with them that the company's new plc status stood for Park Lane Company. Within two months the staffing level grew from fifteen to fifty. He also embarked on a huge TV advertising campaign for *vitahealth.com*, plus a new wave of lavish parties for the London-based media.

Then came the 'dot.com crash'. Panic selling of Internet shares pushed prices down dramatically throughout the world. Shares in *vitahealth.com* fell 77% in just six days. Rupert blessed his good fortune in having raised the extra capital just in time. Yet within a few months he found a different attitude from bankers, potential staff and customers alike. Whereas before he could do no wrong, now he could do nothing right. The media poured scorn on the sports car they had pictured lovingly just a few weeks before, and suddenly Rupert's overdraft level seemed to be the bank's number one priority.

Answers on pages 20–21 Answers on pages 20–21 Answers on pages 20–21

As the company started to turn towards recession, health clubs were less inclined to sign up with *vitahealth.com*. Then regular customers stopped paying their bills on time and – worst of all – some of the more luxurious health clubs went into liquidation, leaving unpaid bills. While others fretted, Rupert was confident that it was no more than a 'little downturn'. He continued to hire graduate programmers on top salaries. His aim had always been to create the ultimate lifestyle web site. This was his chance to do it – while others took the short-sighted view and cut back.

He might have survived had it not been for the hammer blow of the start-up of *Easyleisure.com* – which offered a free listing for every kind of club, cinema and other leisure facility. Rupert was furious at what he claimed was 'grossly unfair competition'. Revenues at *vitahealth.com* started to sink as cancellations flooded in. Rupert responded by dropping charges, but rather too late. Already he had lost one third of his subscriber base. That was when the bank manager phoned to say that unless the £1 million overdraft was settled within 24 hours, the company would be liquidated.

A few frantic hours achieved little. Phone calls to customers with outstanding debts generated promises, but no actual cash. Rupert bought his sports car from the business 'to inject £20 000 in' and ensured that his company expense bills were settled on his credit card. Two staff asked whether the rumours were true, but Rupert could not bring himself to tell them. When staff arrived for work the following morning, the doors were locked against them. Unemployment was a very abrupt, sad end to such a promising business.

When a journalist interviewed Rupert, some weeks after the collapse of *vitahealth.com* plc, she asked whether he felt responsible for what had happened. He replied:

'What, responsible for creating all those jobs? Responsible for giving people eighteen months of better information about healthy living? Yes, I suppose I do.'

1 Explain the business significance of the following terms:

   (a) 'plc status' (line 31) [5]

   (b) 'unfair competition' (line 51). [5]

2 Discuss the key features of a successful start-up for a business such as *vitahealth.com*. [15]

3 It could be argued that Rupert's business objectives were unusually focused upon his lifestyle rather than profit. Discuss whether Rupert's stakeholders would have been better served by a tighter focus upon profit. [15]

[AQA, January 2001]

Answers

(1) (a) *Knowledge*

Plc status signifies that the company is a public limited company, with share capital exceeding £50 000, and is able to advertise and sell its shares to the public via the stock market. **(1–2 marks)**

Understanding/Application

- Access to the public will make it easier to raise more cash for expansion.
- More pressure may be put on the managers of the business for short-term profits at the expense of long-term growth.
- It is more likely that managers and owners will have different priorities – 'divorce of ownership and control'. **(3–5 marks)**

(b) *Knowledge*

Unfair competition can refer to anti-competitive practices, including collusion between firms, setting prices below cost with the intention of destroying the competition, spreading untrue rumours about competitors. **(1–2 marks)**

Understanding/Application

- The consumer loses out in the long-term due to higher prices and/or a lack of choice.
- Ultimately reduced competition leads to inefficiency in firms and hence higher costs and prices.
- Any firm found guilty of unfair competition can be fined substantial amounts by the UK and EU competition authorities. **(3–5 marks)**

(2) *Knowledge*

Key features for a successful start-up include:
- The location of the business.
- The raising of sufficient and appropriate finance.
- Building up and keeping a good customer base.
- An innovative idea that leads to a business opportunity that can be protected.
- The right workforce which is well trained and motivated. **(1–3 marks)**

Understanding/Application

Location is not an issue for *vitahealth.com*, as an Internet-based business does not have a physical presence for the customer. Whether the business is based in London, Birmingham or Glasgow will not affect the accessibility for the customer.
Rupert successfully raised £50 million pounds, which should provide ample cash to set up a company such as this. **(4–6 marks)**

Analysis

It could be argued that *vitahealth.com* did not take action to maintain its customer base after it had very successfully built it up. Could *vitahealth.com* not have offered special pricing deals to encourage regular customers to sign up for a longer term? Given the nature of Rupert's business idea, it was very difficult to protect the idea and prevent other firms from setting up in competition, as *Easyleisure.com* did.
(7–10 marks)

Evaluation

Although the location of the business tied in with the image that Rupert was trying to portray, such an excessive deal as £5 million over 10 years was maybe not appropriate for such a new company. With hindsight, if some of this money had been saved by renting cheaper premises, the firm would not have had the £1 million overdraft that ultimately led to *vitahealth.com*'s demise.

Given this fact it could also be argued that the need for sufficient finance is the most important factor when starting up a business. New firms will always be more susceptible to fluctuations in the business cycle. **(11–15 marks)**

> **examiner's tip**
>
> **Business Studies does not usually contain right and wrong answers. For example, an argument could be made that any one of the key features is the most important. The essential point is that your answer should justify why you think a particular factor is most important, using relevant evidence.**

(3) *Knowledge*

Stakeholders include the banks, employees, customers and shareholders. Business objectives may be related to costs, revenue, sales and market share in addition to profit. **(1–3 marks)**

Understanding/Application

Rupert was apparently more concerned about image than business sense. His unnecessarily expensive company car and lavish parties will have put a large burden on the company's cash flow situation, as well as profit levels. If Rupert had paid more attention to the profit motive it could be argued that greater focus on cost controls would have been present and on building business success based upon customer loyalty rather than press hype. **(4–6 marks)**

Analysis

Customers would have benefited from less extravagance and therefore lower costs. When the recession arrived, if the company had been concentrating more on profit it may have looked at changing company policy to better serve the customers. For example, lower pricing may have allowed the leisure clubs to reduce their costs in turn, so ensuring a better chance of success for both them and *vitahealth.com*. Rupert's objective of taking £6 million for himself out of the share issue should be questioned. This money was vital for ploughing into the company's start-up. The 10-year lease for plush offices in Park Lane was also a questionable business decision. A company more focused on profit would not have agreed to such an expensive and long-term business deal at that stage of the company's development. Why does a company that has no direct dealings with its customers need to be located in such an expensive part of the country? **(7–10 marks)**

Evaluation

The pursuit of long-term profits should have been Rupert's aim, instead of short-term indulgences such as parties and expensive cars. Although the latter may well have created a particular image for the company this was very much for the benefit of the press. However, the customers would not benefit from this in the long-run. The lavish offices may have been very nice for the employees to work in, giving them pleasant surroundings, which may have added to their motivation. However, these benefits cannot be offset against the tremendous expense involved. As was seen in the long-run, the frivolous expenses contributed to the terminal decline of the business. The employees have lost their jobs, so that any benefits they did receive initially have been quite clearly exceeded by the long-term problem of finding themselves unemployed. **(11–15 marks)**

Chapter 3

Structure and growth

Questions with model answers

Staff concerns at Bakers plc

Robert Short is the recently appointed Managing Director of Bakers plc, a biscuit manufacturer employing one hundred and fifty workers. He is concerned about sales and profits and is keen to introduce performance-related pay for all workers in the firm. In order to test reactions to this he asked a number of managers to seek out opinions informally among the workers. Not everyone was pleased at the suggestion.

Production workers felt that they would earn more from such a scheme. On the other hand, the sales team, who have always earned more than production workers, feared that performance-related pay, combined with growing competition in the biscuit market, could leave them worse off.

When Robert took over as Managing Director his salary was highly publicised and this caused quite a bit of resentment among workers. Any decision he makes which affects company wages will almost certainly attract criticism.

Robert decided to push ahead with the performance-related pay scheme. His autocratic leadership style had achieved results in his previous posts. Now would be no different. He was convinced that Bakers plc would benefit in the long term.

Examiner's Commentary

For help see Revise AS Study Guide pp. 50–51

(a) (i) What are the differences between formal and informal methods of communication? [2]

(ii) Outline **two** advantages and **two** disadvantages of using an informal method of communication in this situation. [4]

(b) What other strategies, apart from performance-related pay, could be employed in Bakers plc to improve the performance of the sales team? [8]

(c) Evaluate whether or not the Managing Director should consider changing his leadership style to one which is more democratic. [16]

[CCEA, 2000]

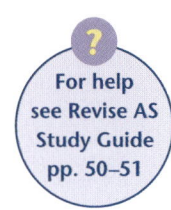

C grade candidate – mark scored 15/30

(a) (i) Formal communication goes along the chain of command. Informal communication doesn't.

(ii) Informal communication tends to be quick. Secondly, it can be helpful to some staff because the language is less formal. The first disadvantage is that it is unofficial. Secondly, because it is unofficial, staff can ignore it.

(b) I would suggest the firm examines the use of sales bonuses or commission. These are valuable incentives for sales staff, because they are motivated financially to sell the firm's products. As a result they are likely to be happier in their work, knowing that more sales will achieve more money in their pay packets. Other strategies for the firm include improving the working lot of the sales staff, e.g. taking account of what Maslow suggests is important: self-esteem and self-actualisation. This means that the managers should give the sales staff the opportunity to achieve what they want to achieve, and to recognise their contributions to the work of the firm.

(c) Many people now recognise that an autocratic approach to leadership can bring as many problems as it solves. It means that the manager takes full control of the decision-making process, and this has the weakness that others are not involved. Although decisions are taken quickly, the fact that the manager may not consult with others means that the decision is more likely to be a wrong one. Most people enjoy taking on responsibility (e.g. McGregor and his 'Theory Y' person), and an autocratic leadership style denies them the chance.

The democratic approach would involve all staff to a greater extent and support the manager's decision-making so I would support the idea of a change. Involvement means motivation, and motivation means better quality and quantity of output.

Examiner's Commentary

Although there are relatively few marks for **(a)**, these answers are much too brief at AS level: the points made need more description and explanation.

Including references to bonuses and commissions is incorrect: the question states 'apart from performance-related pay'. Candidates who spend time including inappropriate detail penalise themselves.

The candidate has considered several implications of an autocratic leadership style, but has not realised that there are other factors that help determine the most appropriate style.

GRADE BOOSTER

The answer to **(c)** should relate more closely to the case study by using information given about the departments and the numbers employed.

A grade candidate – mark scored 28/30

Examiner's Commentary

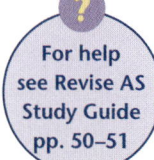

For help see Revise AS Study Guide pp. 50–51

(a) (i) Formal communication takes place through the organisation's hierarchy, and is officially recognised and accepted by all staff. Informal communication is unofficial, flowing 'through the grapevine' and not being formally recognised by those (especially managers) in the organisation.

(ii) Two advantages are: first, that informal communication can expand and further explain a formal communication: this may be necessary in this situation; second, it is an inexpensive method of communication, normally less expensive than a formal one. One disadvantage is that, because it is informal, the information may become changed and inaccurate: second, it can reinforce a feeling amongst staff that management is either distant, incompetent, or both.

The answer to part (a) contains more relevant information than the answer on page 23, and is worth full marks.

(b) In financial terms, the team could be offered additional 'perks' (fringe benefits) or, if appropriate, membership of a share scheme or profit-sharing scheme, neither of which is normally classified as 'performance-related pay' at this level of employment. Management should also consider Herzberg's motivators and hygiene factors, such as increasing promotion opportunities for the sales team, improvements to their work environment, and a review of their work to ensure it is interesting and motivational. The status of their work should also be acknowledged, to encourage motivation.

The sales team's performance could also be improved by looking 'outside' their immediate department. For example, a review of the firm's communication policy and procedures could improve sales performance, together with an evaluation of the quality of the firm's products, an audit of the physical resources it provides for the sales team, and a review of the quality of market and other information available to them.

A well-analysed approach, identifying a range of relevant factors.

(c) The autocratic approach of a manager such as Robert Short has a number of advantages. It means that he retains control over decision-making, which is therefore likely to be carried out quickly and consistently. As a result, Bakers plc should be able to respond quickly to changing market conditions.

Although Robert Short would probably find it difficult with 150 employees under him to adopt a democratic approach to leadership and management, there are a number of benefits associated with the democratic approach. It is usually regarded as a more motivating leadership or management style, since through greater participation in decision-making employees become more involved in the business. As a result, there is improved communication, which includes effective communication of the business objectives: this can also motivate employees, since they know they are involved in helping to achieve these objectives. There is often less need for supervision if a democratic leadership style is adopted, with teams working more closely together towards achieving business objectives.

The question asks you to 'evaluate', and so a balanced answer is required. This answer outlines the benefits of both autocratic and democratic management styles, and argues (correctly) that there is not necessarily a right answer.

A grade continued

There is no one right answer as to the style of leadership that any manager should adopt. The most appropriate style of leadership depends on a number of factors. These include the culture and history of the firm (it isn't clear whether Bakers plc has a tradition of autocratic leadership, although Robert Short was appointed presumably in the knowledge he had an autocratic style), and the manager's own personality (it is clear that Robert Short believes in the autocratic approach). Other factors include the nature and size of the staff, and the depth of the organisational structure/hierarchy: with 150 staff, the company is probably medium-sized, and seems to have a functional structure.

The evidence is largely inconclusive. I would suggest that Robert Short should consider changing his style if friction continues. The strengths of the democratic approach are increasingly recognised by management theorists, and to continue adopting an autocratic approach simply because it has worked in other positions is not sufficient evidence in itself that it will work in Bakers plc.

Examiner's Commentary

This is an excellent example of how case-study information can be applied to the question topic.

A well-structured conclusion with a suitable suggestion based on the earlier arguments.

Exam practice questions

1 Bitza Ltd is currently producing 200 units per month. Its fixed costs are £1000 per month and its variable costs are £5.50 per unit. The table below shows its fixed and variable costs per month at five different levels of output:

OUTPUT (Units per month)	FC (£ per month)	VC (£ per month)
200	1000	1100
300	1000	1500
400	1800	2000
500	1800	2500
600	1800	2700

(a) Calculate Total Cost, Average Variable Cost and Average Cost at each level of output. [5]

(b) Using your calculations and the information in the table above, examine how this firm could best gain from economies of scale. [8]

(c) **(i)** Outline the ways in which Bitza Ltd may benefit from external economies of scale. [4]

(ii) Apart from economies of scale, evaluate the impact of growth on a small business. [13]

[CCEA, 1999]

2 **SPORTSMANIA HOTS UP PACE WITH FRANCHISES**

David Hoskins has developed a chain of sports stores, called Sportsmania, located on industrial estates. He is a discount retailer selling sports gear at bargain prices. Sportsmania is five years old and already has sales of £12 million. In 1997 he started looking at franchises and now twelve of his eighteen outlets are franchised out. Hoskins spent £25 000 in the first six months on his search for franchise applicants and still spends £20 000 a year to attract franchisees. He has refined his selection technique and now insists that applicants come and work with him for a week before he agrees to sign them up.

(a) Briefly explain the term *franchise*. [2]

(b) Evaluate the view that creating franchises is a sound method of expanding the business of Sportsmania. [6]

[WJEC, January 2002]

3 When the directors of Roadshow, Promotions and Marketing (RPM) started out, their policy was to keep main resources in-house in order to encourage a team approach. The business has now grown to a point where the directors have lost touch with all the details and need to delegate some responsibility.

Summary of Roadshow, Promotions and Marketing (RPM) sales and activities

Total Sales	Business Activity	Note
70%	Planning and staging shows	
23%	Field marketing accounts obtained	Lower level of profits
7%	Photographic and creative services e.g. web design	Provides 10% of profit

The directors are considering restructuring into the different business activities identified in the table above, which would reflect the trends. This would simplify the sales process and managers of each unit would be free to develop new businesses in their area rather than having to think about the total package.

Source: adapted from 'To split or not to split – that is the question for an event manager?':
The Sunday Times, 20 May 2001.

(a) Assess the benefits and drawbacks to RPM of adopting a matrix structure for its business. [8]

(b) Evaluate **one** method RPM might use to motivate its staff during this restructuring. [10]

(c) Analyse the ways in which communication is an important issue, apart from in terms of motivation, if the proposed changes to RPM go ahead. [8]

[Edexcel, January 2003]

Answers

(1) (a)

Output (units/month)	Fixed costs (£/month)	Variable costs (£/month)	Total costs (£/month)	Average variable costs (£/unit)	Average costs (£/unit)
200	1000	1100	2100	5.50	10.50
300	1000	1500	2500	5.00	8.33
400	1800	2000	3800	5.00	9.50
500	1800	2500	4300	5.00	8.60
600	1800	2700	4500	4.50	7.50

(b) *Knowledge*

- The workings show that Bitza Ltd gains from economies of scale. This is at an output of 300 units per month. **(1–2 marks)**

Application/Understanding

- If Bitza Ltd increases output to 400 a month, its average costs rise to £9.50 per unit. This is the result of the additional £800 fixed costs (this is a 'stepped' cost).
- Now the 'step' has occurred, presumably due to full capacity at this output, average costs again fall continually to 600 units/month (£7.50 per unit).
- This is due to the lower unit variable costs, e.g. through bulk-buying. **(3–5 marks)**

Analysis

- If the company can produce and sell at this level, it will pay to do so in terms of this cost analysis.
- Its difficulty will be increasing its sales to match the increased output: any drop in the unit selling price may negate the benefits from lower unit costs. **(6–8 marks)**

(c) (i) *Knowledge*

- External economies of scale arise from a growth in the size of the industry.
- All firms in the industry will benefit from these economies. **(1–2 marks)**

Application/Understanding

- Bitza Ltd may gain from external economies of concentration.
- If it is a firm in a locally-based industry, it will benefit from having suitably skilled employees living in the locality.
- There is also the nearness of support firms supplying it with materials and other resources, the positive image or reputation associated with the local area (e.g. 'Potteries china', 'Sheffield steel'), and local providers offering training courses relevant to its industry.
- Another commonly found external economy relates to information: Bitza Ltd may gain from locally-based or locally-available sources of information and advice.
- These all help lower the firm's average cost. **(3–4 marks)**

(ii) *Knowledge*
- Growth will affect a small business in both positive and negative ways.
- Perhaps the two greatest benefits from growth are profit and recognition. **(1–2 marks)**

Application/Understanding
- Profit comes from the growth in sales, assuming the business keeps its profitability (i.e. net profit margin remains roughly constant).
- This profit will help support additional growth.
- Recognition brings with it potential for more business in the form of extra sales/work, and – as the firm grows – this greater amount of work will require the firm to increase its productive or other capacity.
- In turn, the greater capacity allows the firm to take on larger and more lucrative contracts. **(3–5 marks)**

examiner's tip The question does not refer to Bitza Ltd, so your answer can be based on small firms in general.

Analysis
- Once the firm has grown beyond the accepted size of being 'small' (two from: turnover above £2.8 million, balance sheet total above £1.4 million, average employees over 50), it loses exemption from filing disclosures and may also lose additional government help.
- The original owners may have to relinquish some or all control due to the need for additional finance and/or a more complex organisational structure.
- This may lead to a different organisational culture developing, and the loss of the 'personal touch' often closely associated with smaller firms. **(6–9 marks)**

Evaluation
- Eventually the firm may reach a size at which diseconomies of scale start outweighing the economies of scale from growth.
- Overall, the benefits of growth may well exceed the negative impact from the point of view of both owners and staff.
- Survival is also more likely once the firm has grown. **(10–13 marks)**

examiner's tip Remember you need to write a valid conclusion to gain marks for evaluation.

(2) (a) *Knowledge and Application/Understanding*
- A franchisor (the business owning the franchise) sells the rights to other businesses (franchisees) to sell its products. Examples include some 'fast-food' outlets, such as many McDonald's outlets. **(2 marks)**

(b) *Knowledge* and *Application/Understanding*
- Franchising allows Sportsmania to expand its business without substantial capital investment.
- The franchisees are likely to pay capital set-up costs, and will also pay royalties to Sportsmania. **(1–2 marks)**

Analysis
- Sportsmania should still be in control of the franchise, and can therefore withdraw it if necessary.
- It will receive royalties regularly, which are likely to be based on turnover. **(3–4 marks)**

Evaluation
- Sportsmania relies to a large extent on the quality of its franchisees, so it is not fully in control of its market.
- Working with prospective franchisees reduces the risk of recruiting poor ones.
- Although it is costly to recruit franchisees, it is a sound investment because one badly performing franchisee can affect the whole business. **(5–6 marks)**

> **examiner's tip** Be careful to use the terms *franchisor* and *franchisee* correctly.

(3) (a) *Knowledge*
- A matrix structure is associated with a task culture that is job or project oriented.
- It attempts to avoid the problems associated with more traditional and formal structures, where senior managers become isolated from other levels. **(1–2 marks)**

Application/Understanding
- A matrix structure could be suitable for RPM because '… the directors have lost touch with all the details …'.
- It should allow the business to co-ordinate its various projects more efficiently. **(3–4 marks)**

Analysis
- If RPM continues to face change, a matrix structure can help it keep up-to-date through its flexibility.
- If RPM is structured to have a wide span of control and not many levels in its hierarchy, a matrix structure should work well. **(5–6 marks)**

Evaluation
- A matrix structure can lack clear lines of responsibility and communication.
- There appear to be a number of likely overlaps between the three areas mentioned in the table.
- This can lead to pressure on staff, who may feel their loyalty is divided between more than one manager. **(7–8 marks)**

(b) *Knowledge*
- There are a number of different strategies available to RPM.
- These include: increasing pay or other financial rewards, encouraging internal promotion, training schemes, job enrichment. **(1–2 marks)**

Application/Understanding
- Increased pay is one way to motivate RPM staff.
- Whilst pay is not the only means to motivate staff, many theorists recognise its fundamental importance. **(3–4 marks)**

Analysis
- Increasing pay would add to the costs of RPM.
- It should, however, encourage staff to face the changes that are being made in the structure. **(5–6 marks)**

Evaluation
- As a result of the pay increase, staff should feel more valued, more secure, and therefore more motivated.
- RPM should still support any pay increase with further ways to motivate its staff during the restructuring.
- Increased pay on its own will not necessarily fully motivate all staff.
- For example, it will be important to keep staff fully informed of changes in the structure. **(7–10 marks)**

> **examiner's tip** Whatever motivational method is selected, be prepared to explain that RPM would benefit from using a range of appropriate motivational approaches, both financial and non-financial.

(c) *Knowledge*
- Efficient communication is vital to all businesses.
- Poor communication leads to misunderstandings, and can affect production and sales performances. **(1–3 marks)**

Application/Understanding
- RPM will need to communicate the changes as they occur.
- Failure to do so is likely to demotivate RPM staff, who as a result will feel undervalued. **(4–6 marks)**

Analysis
- 70% of RPM's work is with planning and staging shows, so communication with its clients is obviously crucial to maintain customer satisfaction.
- Internally, RPM staff will need efficient communication to put the changes into practice, and to support each other in this time of change. **(7–8 marks)**

> **examiner's tip** Although this is the final part of the question, it is the easiest in that it is restricted to Level 3 (Analysis) only.

Chapter 4

External influences

Questions with model answers

Ice cream from Mars

In the late 1980s, Walls ice cream stood as the established market leader. It must have appeared to Walls that its position could not be threatened. However, food technology was changing fast. By 1988 the market had seen the transformation of chocolate confectionery into ice cream bars; by 1995 it was the fastest growing sector of the ice cream market. Mars were the first company to launch an ice cream version of a popular chocolate bar.

However, Mars found it difficult to enter the market, as Walls and Lyons Maid was supplying freezers free of charge to small retailers on condition that they stock only their ice cream in the cabinet. The owners of Walls, Unilever, sought to prevent Mars from entering the market and they began legal proceedings against Mars alleging that they had induced retailers to break their exclusive contracts with Walls. Eventually, Mars went to the European Commission in 1991 accusing Unilever of illegal anti-competitive practices. In October 1992, the UK's Office of Fair Trading also announced an investigation into freezer exclusivity in the UK.

In March 1994 the Monopolies and Mergers Commission found that exclusivity did not prevent competition from working. However, one year later the European Commission condemned freezer exclusivity, saying that it resulted in the restriction of competition, and so infringed Articles 85 and 86 of the EC Treaty. Eventually, the European Commission decided that the practice of freezer exclusivity was illegal throughout the EU.

Source: adapted from *The Times 100 Case Studies*, 1995 and the *Financial Times*, 10 June, 1999

Examiner's Commentary

For help see Revise AS Study Guide pp. 68–70

(a) Use the article to outline the role of the Monopolies and Mergers Commission (now called the Competition Commission). **[4]**

(b) Explain the meaning of the phrase 'restriction of competition'. **[4]**

(c) Analyse how the ending of freezer exclusivity may have affected Walls. **[8]**

(d) Discuss what other consumer protection law may affect the way in which Mars and Walls operate. **[10]**

C grade candidate – mark scored 13/26

Examiner's Commentary

(a) To ensure that large companies do not exploit their customers, the Competition Commission has the power to investigate any situation where they feel that a company that has more than 25% of the market either through growth or merger, is acting in an uncompetitive manner.

Although this is a good explanation of the role of the Competition Commission, it does not link with the evidence available in the article.

(b) The phrase 'restriction of competition' is referring to the fact that a company can act in such a way that true competition cannot take place, so affecting the consumer. In the ice cream industry there are a few large firms controlling the market, so competition may be prevented.

If this last comment had been explained then full marks would have been awarded.

(c) The ending of freezer exclusivity will have affected Walls in a major way. It will have meant that they faced more competition from Mars and other companies. If shops are now able to put any company's ice cream in their freezers, Walls will find that customers will have more choice when making a purchase. This will mean that Walls will probably have to reduce their price to compete. This will affect Walls' position in the market, with a likely fall in market share.

This is a good start to an answer, but could have so easily been developed for many more marks. What about the effect of falling sales on their profits; how may this have affected their employment levels; what might Walls have done about this?

(d) Both Mars and Walls will have to comply with many other regulations protecting the consumer. One is the Trade Descriptions Act, which makes it illegal to give a wrong or misleading description of their ice cream. The Food Safety Act ensures that the ice cream sold is fit for human consumption The Unsolicited Goods Act prevents consumers from demanding payment for goods received that they have not requested. The Weights and Measures Act ensures that the tubs of ice cream sold are of the correct weight.

This is a poor answer, for two reasons. First, there is no direct reference to the companies in the case study. Just occasionally mentioning the words ice cream does not qualify for much context. Second, to include The Unsolicited Goods Act is nonsensical as it would be unlikely to find ice cream being sent through the post!

External influences

GRADE BOOSTER

The number of marks available for each question gives a good indication of how much to write.

A grade candidate – mark scored 26/26

Examiner's Commentary

(a) The Competition Commission is a government organisation that checks that when legal monopolies (more than 25% of the market) exist they are not against the public interest. They investigated the Walls case because there may have been a case of them abusing their position in the market. It may be argued that not allowing stores to put other firms' products into their freezers was anti-competitive, as most shops would not have room to have more than one freezer and so would not be able to stock Mars' products.

The role of the Competition Commission is clearly outlined **and** is referring specifically to the context.

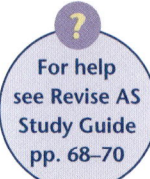

For help see Revise AS Study Guide pp. 68–70

(b) Under UK and EU law, firms must not act in a way that prevents free competition from taking place. It is expected that firms should not try to take unfair advantage of their dominant position in the market – for example, by putting undue pressure on retailers to stock their product. If this is allowed to happen, the resulting lack of competition may mean that prices are higher than they should be and there will be less choice for the consumer. This is likely to happen if the stores only stock Walls' products. The lack of choice will adversely affect customers and will allow Walls to charge a higher price as there is little likelihood that customers will shop around for this particular product since ice cream is usually bought on impulse.

Probably too full an answer for only 4 marks, but there is no doubt the student knows what they are talking about.

(c) The ending of freezer exclusivity may have had a major effect on the operation of Walls. The main effect will have been the ending of Walls' monopolistic position in the market. Now that the shops can stock other brands of ice cream in their freezers, the major competitors such as Mars will have freer access to more retail outlets. This will affect the sales of Walls' ice cream, as they will no longer have such guaranteed levels of sales. This will potentially affect their profits and may mean that Walls will have to look at other ways of marketing their product. It may also be the case that jobs will be lost within the Walls organisation, as fewer sales and support staff are needed to support lower sales output.

A solid coverage of the main points so far.

However, given the fact that Walls has held such a dominant position in the market for so long, they may find that even with increased competition they are able to take advantage of the brand loyalty built up over the previous years. This would suggest that as long as they still continue to provide freezers free of charge to retailers, with Walls' advertising on the outside, they will only see a small fall in sales.

Analysis achieved by questioning the likelihood of the most obvious scenario happening.

External influences

A grade continued

Examiner's Commentary

(d) One law that will have a huge effect on any ice cream company is the Food Safety Act. It requires that food is safe for consumption, is of the quality stated and the description does not mislead the consumer.

For example, the freezers provided must ensure that the ice cream is kept at an appropriate temperature so that the product does not melt and potentially create health problems. Also, a Lemon Sorbet lolly should actually be lemon flavoured and should be sorbet rather than ice cream.

This kind of issue is also covered under the Trade Descriptions Act, which requires that goods offered for sale do not have misleading descriptions. An ice cream Snickers bar would be expected to contain peanuts, as they are vital ingredients in a standard Snickers chocolate bar.

The weight of an ice cream must conform to that printed on its wrapper. This is covered by the Weights and Measures Act, which makes it an offence to sell goods underweight or short in quantity.

The failure to abide by these laws could seriously undermine the future success of Walls or Mars. The bad publicity attracted from breaking any of these laws could affect their sales. (This has happened recently to Perrier and Coca-Cola.) It will lead to a fall in consumer confidence, which may lead to a complete collapse in demand not just for ice creams but other products as well. Both Walls and Mars are involved in many other food products, and if the consumer loses faith in one product it may lead to a fall in demand for all products made by that company. Given the fact that Walls and Mars are both operating in what is now a very competitive market, one publicised case of breaking the law may provide an opportunity for a competitor to take a larger market share, which may be very difficult to regain.

A good start. Straightaway the candidate is showing that they are only going to select the laws that affect ice cream.

A good answer that selects the appropriate laws for this case and then discusses the implications of not abiding by them. Good recognition that any slip-up by Mars or Walls will have a potential long-term effect in such a competitive market.

External influences

Exam practice questions

DECISION TIME AT J & M TAYLOR

J & M Taylor Ltd is a family-run business based in the north east of England. The business is still owned and run by the founders, John and Mary Taylor. Their two children, Robert and Joanne, joined the business after leaving university in 1990 and 1993 respectively. In addition to the four family members, the business also employs 12 other people who are employed in the production of the various products on which the business has built its reputation over the last 20 years.

The business is a supplier of ingredients, such as buns, salads, and potatoes, required by the fast food industry. From the start, it has been company policy to supply a large range of products in order that they could appeal to as wide a customer base as possible. This policy has been very successful so far and the company supplies a wide variety of outlets, varying from fish and chip shops to the more fashionable types of outlet such as tapas bars.

The North East has recently experienced the loss of a large number of jobs in the textile and electronics industries pushing the unemployment rate in the area to approximately 8%. Many people in the region were beginning to economise and were cutting down on any unnecessary expenditure. One of the sectors feeling the pressure from such cuts was the take-away food industry with most outlets reporting a noticeable drop in trade. J & M Taylor Ltd was no exception; over the last eight weeks Robert had reported a 10% drop in orders from regular customers.

These changes in the local economy have led the family to consider setting up a totally new business that would, hopefully, take advantage of the current fashion for eating organic food. They were considering calling this new venture 'Freshers' and its mission would be to provide high quality snacks using only organic produce. Joanne had been consciously buying organic food whenever she could for almost five years now and was therefore aware of the range of food that was available and its price. She had done some market research and had found that there was not a single cafe in the area that was offering organic food. Therefore she was convinced that although the take-away and cafe businesses in the region were seeing a downturn in sales, a new venture promising only pure and wholesome food would attract sufficient people to make the business profitable. Her main problem was that she needed to persuade the rest of the family that setting up a new business at this time was not foolish and was likely to succeed. She emphasised that, although the business cycle was experiencing a downturn at the moment, the family should be prepared for the upturn which would, hopefully, follow.

The family decided to hold a business meeting to discuss the options open to them in order to ensure the company's survival. Robert suggested that before the meeting each of them should do a SWOT analysis of the business and they would then have a foundation on which to base their discussion.

Answers on pages 39–43 Answers on pages 39–43 Answers on pages 39–43

During the meeting it became clear that they had two main options available to them. They could reduce their workforce until demand began to increase again or they could try Joanne's idea and start a new business based on organic snacks. They agreed to go away and to meet again in three days when each of them would have prepared a list of the advantages and disadvantages of both of the proposals. When they met again Mary shocked them all by saying that she had not bothered to consider the two options because, after leaving the first meeting, she had thought of an even better idea. She said that she was convinced that they should concentrate on the business that they have been successful in for the past 20 years and that, instead of risking a totally new business, they should explore the possibility of exporting the products that they currently make and supply. She argued that the reduction in interest rates made this the ideal time for such an experiment. As Mary had not been known for coming up with ideas in the past, she was rather surprised when John, Robert and Joanne all agreed that this was something that could be worth considering. Now they had three options to consider!

During the same period that the job losses and the fall in orders were occurring, interest rates were reduced by a total of 0.75% from 7% to 6.25%. This was thought to be in response to appeals from businesses which said that they could not afford to invest at the higher rates of interest, and that the exchange rate was being pushed up and was reducing their ability to gain export orders.

(a) Explain two ways in which a fall in interest rates can affect a business such as J & M Taylor Ltd. [10]

(b) Evaluate the business opportunities for J & M Taylor Ltd resulting from a future upturn in the business cycle. [15]

[AQA, Specimen]

2 NISSAN UK RISKS MICRA LOSS

As the car industry moved into the new millennium, Nissan threatened to switch production of its next Micra car away from the UK, raising the possibility of thousands more job losses in the motor industry. The Japanese company, like other motor manufacturers, found its profits reduced by the high value of the pound. Nissan revealed the crisis facing its Sunderland factory as Ford announced the end of car production at Dagenham in Essex. Rover has had serious problems for some time.

One of Rover's potential rescuers, the venture capital company Phoenix, defended its business plan for Rover. The plan claimed new models could be developed for under half the £1.2 billion BMW, Rover's previous owners, spent on its new small car. Phoenix head and Rover Chief Executive, John Towers, said he believed investment could double if a partner became involved.

Nissan's Sunderland factory has received substantial financial assistance from the UK government and is Europe's most efficient. Even so, Nissan warned that unless there are further cost reductions of 30% the next Micra will be built in the French and Spanish factories of Renault with whom it has formed a joint venture. The Sunderland factory could lose up to 2000 jobs unless the current production of the Micra is replaced. A further 10 000 UK jobs could be lost at suppliers.

The Nissan Almeira and Primera will continue to be built in Sunderland, but the joint venture would allow the Micra to share major components with the Renault Clio and be produced much more cheaply in the Euro zone.

Nissan UK's Chief Executive recently called for Britain to join the Euro. However, the Chairman of Ford Europe said that Dagenham had lost its car production because it was not as flexible or productive as the company's continental factories. These have more modern facilities so that three or four models can be built on the same assembly line.

Source: adapted from *The Observer*, 14th May 2000

(a) Outline **two** possible examples of social costs that car manufacturing might create. [4]

(b) Analyse the likely reasons why the UK government provided financial assistance to Nissan at its Sunderland factory. [9]

(c) Evaluate the economic factors that are likely to influence the demand for new Nissan cars in the UK. [14]

(d) Evaluate how the UK stakeholders in Nissan might be affected if the new Micra is manufactured abroad. [14]

[Adapted from OCR, January 2002]

examiner's tip These questions should be completed in 55 minutes if attempted under examination conditions.

Answers

examiner's tip — Question 1 makes up half of a 60-minute exam. This means it should take about 30 minutes in total.

(1) (a) *Knowledge*

Any two effects of lower interest rates generally, including:

- Loans will be cheaper
- Companies are more likely to increase investment in capital
- Consumers will be better off as they will find it easier to borrow money
- Opportunity cost of holding stocks will fall. **(1–4 marks)**

Understanding/Application

Clear impact on J & M Taylor is shown, as a result of interest rates falling:

- Because loans are cheaper it will mean that J & M Taylor will find that the cost of developing the organic concept or the exporting side of the business will be cheaper and therefore more attractive.
- Because of the nature of J & M Taylor's business, demand will increase as consumers become better off. A fall in interest rates will lead to consumers buying more non-essential products such as fast food.
- The fall in opportunity cost of holding stocks may lead to production increasing to replenish stocks that have been allowed to dwindle during periods of high interest rates. **(5–10 marks)**

(b) *Knowledge*

The business cycle describes the trend in a country's output (or GDP) over a period of time. Typically, the economy moves through four distinct stages: Boom, Recession, Slump and Recovery. **(1–3 marks)**

Understanding/Application

An upturn in the business cycle will create a number of opportunities, including:

- Increase in orders from customers, both new and old
- Increased demand with no price changes will lead to improved profits
- The business may be encouraged to diversify as confidence in the economy increases
- More investment projects will be investigated. **(4–6 marks)**

Analysis

A clear discussion of the impact on, and reaction of, J & M Taylors. For example:

- Improvements in the business cycle will lead to new fast food outlets opening, which will lead to a greater demand for J & M Taylor's products.
- It becomes easier for companies to expand and introduce new products. Therefore, J & M Taylor may find that it is an ideal opportunity for them to introduce their organic range.
- However, as incomes of customers increase they may be more likely to move 'upmarket' and demand better quality products. This may lead to them consuming less fast food in favour of eating out at 'proper restaurants'.

External influences

- There may be an opportunity for J & M Taylor to diversify and open their own distribution chain, i.e. a retail outlet. This may give them greater control and security over their future business growth. However, they may find the change of sector difficult, due to their lack of knowledge and experience of retailing.

(7–10 marks)

Evaluation

A weighing up of the opportunities available for J & M Taylor, including:

- In the short-run there may be more competition appearing in the market. This will create challenges for a relatively small company. However, their experience and reputation over the last 20 years will give them an advantage against new businesses, especially if they maintain a high level of quality at a reasonable price.
- The new organic venture being considered may give them a unique selling point. Increasing incomes and demands of the customers that may lead them to move 'upmarket' may be met by the provision of the 'Freshers' range of products. This will give J & M Taylor an advantage over the competition.

(11–15 marks)

> **examiner's tip** To gain the best marks you must remember to link the theory to examples discussed in the case study.

(2) (a) *Knowledge*

Any two examples of social costs:

- Destruction of the natural beauty of the land where the car factory is located.
- Air or noise pollution.
- Congestion on the roads adjacent to the plant as employees and suppliers 'get in' and finished cars leave.
- More damage to the local roads. **(1–2 marks)**

Understanding/Application

This requires the answer to show that the candidate knows 'what they are talking about' rather than just listing lots of ideas. For example:

- The damage to the roads will mean that more road repairs are necessary which have to be paid out of the taxes collected from the local population.
- Congestion will add to delays felt by 'third parties' – those people who have no direct involvement in the manufacturing of the cars. **(3–4 marks)**

(b) *Knowledge*

The government wants Nissan to stay in the UK, suppliers may have to close down and more unemployment will be created. **(1–3 marks)**

Understanding/Application

- If Nissan stay in the UK more jobs may be created in the long-term, but also any reduction in the amount of production by Nissan will lead to many job losses at suppliers and related businesses.
- Large numbers of unemployed people will mean that the Government will have to increase spending on benefits and tax receipts will also fall. **(4–7 marks)**

Analysis

A discussion of the consequences for the economy and the government if Nissan leaves the UK.

- A loss of production of cars in the UK will lead to greater demand for imports by the UK population, so worsening the countries' trading position. This may ultimately have an effect on other sectors of industry.
- If the government had not provided financial assistance then ultimately the costs to the UK economy due to lost tax revenues and increase spending on benefits may have been even higher.
- Increased unemployment has been proved to lead to greater social problems, such as crime and social disorder. **(8–9 marks)**

> **examiner's tip**
> There is no need or point in trying to show evaluation in a question that asks you to analyse. There are no marks for evaluation.

(c) *Knowledge*

There are many possible economic factors:

- the price of cars
- the price of substitutes & complements
- the business cycle
- the exchange rate and/or interest rates
- taxation. **(1–3 marks)**

Understanding/Application

- An increase in the price of new Nissan cars will reduce the demand for them.
- If other producers, e.g. Vauxhall, Ford etc., reduce their prices then demand for Nissan cars may fall.
- As many cars are bought using loans or hire purchase agreements, any increase in interest rates may discourage customers from entering these agreements and so demand for cars generally will fall. **(4–6 marks)**

Analysis

- If the exchange rate appreciates then the price of imports will decrease. This will have the effect of increasing the price of UK cars in real terms and so leads to a fall in their demand. In addition, the increased openness of markets in the EU and growing awareness by UK residents of cheaper prices on the continent has added to the demand for imports.
- It is not just the impact of a rising rate of interest on loans and hire purchase agreements. Many consumers in the UK now have a mortgage. Therefore, any increase in interest rates will have a direct effect on their monthly mortgage bill, so reducing the amount of 'spare cash' that consumers have to spend on new cars.
- The increased availability and low prices of second-hand cars may lead to more and more customers in the UK choosing to purchase these rather than new cars. **(7–10 marks)**

> **examiner's tip**
> Good analysis of just two points should be sufficient to gain the maximum 10 marks.

Evaluation

An attempt to sum up the arguments is an easy way of showing evaluation in this particular question. For example:

- Even though the price of new cars has been falling, the increase in running costs, such as petrol prices and car tax, may have a much more significant effect over the lifetime of owning a car.
- However, although the annual costs of running a car are high and increasing, we have still seen a continual rise in the demand for new cars. This may ultimately be due to the increasing income levels of consumers as the economy is in the boom phase of the business cycle and/or the poor standards and availability of public transport across the UK, leaving most individuals with no choice but to use the car for work or social purposes. **(11–14 marks)**

(d) *Knowledge*

Stakeholders include employees, shareholders, customers, suppliers, the government and competitors. **(1–3 marks)**

> **examiner's tip** A common mistake is for students to confuse 'stakeholders' and 'shareholders'.

Understanding/Application

How are the stakeholders interested? For example:

- Employees will be concerned about losing their jobs.
- Shareholders will want to know how the value of their shares and any future dividends will be affected.
- Customers are merely interested whether the price or availability and choice will be affected. **(4–6 marks)**

Analysis

What will be the response of, or impact on, stakeholders? For example:

- A loss of confidence by shareholders who question the business sense of Nissan's decision to move abroad may lead to shareholders selling their shares. This will lead to a fall in Nissan's share price, which may have implications for Nissan's future business security, e.g. the ability to raise finance.
- If the move abroad by Nissan leads to lower prices then customers will be pleased. Increased competitiveness of Nissan cars will lead to increased demand from customers.
- UK based suppliers will fear that they will lose business as Nissan will look to source components locally. Ultimately this may lead to redundancies and even liquidation for the supplier.
- Competitors will feel under greater threat if the move abroad reduces Nissan's costs and prices. Alternatively, customers who want to buy UK-produced cars may switch to these competitors. **(7–10 marks)**

Evaluation

In this sort of question, evaluation is best shown by weighing up the impact on the different stakeholders. For example:

- Loss of business and jobs, including lost business for local suppliers, may cause a downturn for the local community with many attendant problems. The area may appear unattractive to other firms, encouraging them to leave also and/or discouraging them from moving to the area.
- Although it may appear that customers will benefit from lower prices, if those customers rely on the car industry for their income they will be worse off overall.
- Ultimately, the government will see a negative impact on the financial situation in the locality and the country overall, which explains why they are prepared to spend millions of pounds in financial assistance to prevent Nissan from leaving the UK. **(11–14 marks)**

Chapter 5

Accounting and finance

Questions with model answers

The accounts of John Andrews

John Andrews has been in business for three years.
The following figures were taken from his firm's balance sheet.

	£
Equipment and Fittings	2 000
Closing Stock	7 000
Debtors	1 500
Bank	500
Creditors	400
Owner's Capital	10 000
Retained Profit	600

(a) **(i)** Present this information in the form of a vertical balance sheet. [6]

(ii) Explain the term 'working capital'. [2]

(iii) State John Andrews' working capital. [1]

(iv) State the value of John Andrews' Net Assets. [1]

(b) John's accountant values his stock at cost price but John wants to value his stock at selling price. Use your knowledge and understanding of current accounting concepts and standards to advise John if valuing stock at selling price is acceptable. [6]

(c) Evaluate the usefulness of final accounts to the various stakeholders of a public limited company. [14]

[CCEA, 1999]

Examiner's Commentary

For help see Revise AS Study Guide pp. 76–81

C grade candidate – mark scored 15/30

(a) (i) Balance Sheet   £   £

  Fixed assets
   Equipment and fittings   2 000

  Current assets
   Stocks   7 000
   Debtors   1 500
   Bank   500
        9 000

  Current liabilities
   Creditors   400
             8 600
             10 600

  Capital   10 000
   Profit   600
             10 600

(ii) 'Working capital' is current assets less current liabilities.

(iii) John Andrews has £8 600 working capital.

(iv) Net assets are £9 000.

(b) This means John Andrews will be accepting that profit has been made before the stock is sold. This is not allowed by prudence, which is one of the accounting concepts. As a result, John Andrews cannot value his stock at selling price because there is no guarantee it will be sold.

(c) The main stakeholders for public limited companies are interested in two main aspects of the company: its profits and its liquidity. The final accounts are the profit and loss account and balance sheet, and between them these show profit and liquidity (for example, working capital).

Profits are important when the stakeholders want to check the value of their investment, or whether they are going to get a good return as dividend or interest payments. Liquidity will be important to stakeholders lending money to the plc, because they will want their money back at some stage. They will also want the plc to make profits, because they want to be paid interest.

Examiner's Commentary

The heading should read 'Balance Sheet as at ...'.

Although accurate, some labelling is abbreviated or omitted, notably the name of the owner and the descriptions 'net current assets' and 'net assets'.

The candidate hasn't explained what working capital is, but has simply stated how it is calculated.

This is incorrect: the candidate has selected 'current assets' in error.

An accurate, but limited, statement. There is no mention of SSAP 9, and the prudence concept has not been explained fully.

'Profit' is mentioned, but stakeholders are normally more interested in measuring profit against capital employed or turnover, i.e. 'profitability' for the plc. Stakeholders are not identified: this omission makes producing a structured and logical answer more difficult.

Accounting and finance

GRADE BOOSTER

'Stakeholders' vary in type and importance from business to business. Because of this it is not normally sufficient at either AS or A2 level to refer to 'stakeholders' in such general terms.

A grade candidate – mark scored 29/30

Examiner's Commentary

For help see Revise AS Study Guide pp. 76–81

(a) (i) <u>John Andrews: Balance Sheet as at ……</u>

	£	£
Fixed assets		
Equipment and fittings		2 000
Current assets		
Stocks	7 000	
Debtors	1 500	
Bank	500	
	9 000	
Current liabilities		
Creditors	400	
Net current assets		8 600
Net assets		10 600
Financed by:		
Owner's capital		10 000
Net profit		600
		10 600

This is a more fully labelled Balance Sheet. Note the use of important terms such as 'Net current assets', 'Net assets', and 'Financed by'.

(ii) 'Working capital' is the excess of current assets over current liabilities, and indicates John's ability to meet short-term debts as they fall due.

The question asks for an explanation, not merely a statement of how working capital is calculated.

(iii) John has £8600 working capital: £9000 current assets – £400 current liabilities.

(iv) Net assets are £10 600.

Good, workings are shown: this is always important with numerical questions.

Following the vertical layout gives this answer, as well as that to (a) (iii).

(b) John cannot value stock at selling price, because this is against the concept of prudence (sometimes known as conservatism). This concept states that, where different valuations are possible, a business must select the one giving the most cautious presentation of its financial state. This basically means 'always anticipate a loss but never anticipate a profit'. This is reinforced by SSAP 9, which states that stock should be valued at the lower of cost or net realisable value. This means, therefore, that John Andrews will not be allowed to value his stock at selling price, because it would be anticipating a profit, and is also not allowed by SSAP 9.

The candidate might also have added a comment that profits are only recognised when they are actually made – i.e. when the stock is sold.

A grade continued

(c) A plc has many stakeholders. Some of these are internal to the firm - for example, the employees and managers - and others are external. External stakeholders include shareholders, the government (e.g. HM Customs & Excise in connection with VAT), customers, suppliers and lenders. Internally, employees will be interested in the plc's liquidity, since it needs sufficient liquid assets to survive and employ staff. They may also be interested in its profitability, especially if they have a direct interest, e.g. through a profit-sharing scheme. Managers will also be interested in liquidity, as well as judging its success internally (i.e. checking profitability or other trends against past accounting records) and externally (assessing performance against competitors): the final accounts form the basis for this analysis.

Externally, shareholders will be interested in the plc's profitability and overall performance, since this affects (a) the share price and (b) the amount of dividend they will receive. Shareholders use final accounts to judge whether their investment remains worthwhile. Lenders such as banks or debenture holders will want to reassure themselves that their investment in the plc is safe: the evidence comes from analysing its final accounts to see whether it is in a position to pay interest, and also to repay the loans. Suppliers will check the final accounts to assess working capital levels, again to see whether the plc is in a position to pay them. It must be remembered that financial accounts have their limitations - they are historic and need to be compared over time.

The above illustrates that final accounts will be of great interest to all stakeholders of a plc, although the focus of this interest will vary from stakeholder to stakeholder.

Examiner's Commentary

Classifying stakeholders as 'internal' and 'external' has helped to structure the answer. Note, though, that shareholders can also be internal – as well as external – stakeholders.

The opening statement sets the scene by identifying a suitable range of stakeholders, and the final comment summarises and answers the question.

Exam practice questions

1 Dargon Distribution is owned by John Shah. John has just completed his first year of trading and his sister, Velma, is going to help him with his first set of final accounts. Dargon Distribution owns two main fixed assets. Velma has asked John to estimate the working life of each asset and what the scrap value of each might be at the end of that time. John's estimates are set out in the table below.

	Cost Price	Working Life (years)	Estimated Scrap Value
Van	£6000	3	£3000
Computer	£2100	5	£680

(a) Define the term 'depreciation'. [2]

(b) Using **both** the Straight Line and Reducing Balance (at 20%) methods:

　(i) Calculate the depreciation which would be charged each year of the life of each asset. [4]

　(ii) Indicate the net book value at the end of each year of each asset's life. [4]

　(iii) State which method of depreciation John should use, and why. [2]

(c) Evaluate the impact on Dargon Distribution of a decision by John to ignore the depreciation of his fixed assets. [18]

[CCEA, 2000]

Answers on pages 51–54 *Answers* on pages 51–54 *Answers* on pages 51–54

2 These are MacLean plc's summarised financial statements for 2001.

MacLean plc
Profit and loss account for year ended 31 December 2001

	£000
Turnover	1120
Less cost of goods sold	700
Gross profit	420
Less expenses	160
Operating profit	260
Less taxation	65
Profit after tax	195
Less dividends	75
Retained profit	120

MacLean plc
Balance sheet as at 31 December 2001

	£000	£000	£000
Fixed assets (cost)			1380
Total depreciation			465
			915
Current assets:			
Stocks		200	
Debtors		79	
Cash in hand		1	
		280	
Current liabilities:			
Creditors	68		
Taxation	65		
Proposed dividend	75		
Bank overdraft	12		
		220	
Net current assets			60
			975
Capital and reserves:			
Ordinary share capital			600
Share premium			20
Profit & Loss account			355
			975

(a) (i) Identify **two** different stakeholder groups who might have an interest in the financial statements of MacLean plc. [2]

(ii) Analyse why each of these two stakeholder groups might be interested in the company's financial performance. [12]

In the year 2000, MacLean plc made 40% gross profit and 25% net profit margins on its sales. Its return on capital employed was 30%.

(b) Using this information and the financial statements shown above, evaluate the company's overall profitability performance in 2001. [18]

(c) Assess the additional financial and non-financial information needed to make a full evaluation of MacLean plc's performance. [18]

[Edexcel, January 2002]

Answers

(1) (a) *Knowledge*

The fall in value of a fixed asset over a period of time (its useful life), e.g. due to wear and tear, obsolescence or depreciation. **(1–2 marks)**

(b) (i) and **(ii)** *Application/Understanding*

Straight line (Van)

Year	Book value at start	Depreciation	Book value at end
1	6 000	1 000	5 000
2	5 000	1 000	4 000
3	4 000	1 000	3 000

Straight line (Computer)

Year	Book value at start	Depreciation	Book value at end
1	2 100	284	1 816
2	1 816	284	1 532
3	1 532	284	1 248
4	1 248	284	964
5	964	284	680

Reducing balance (Van)

Year	Book value at start	Depreciation	Book value at end
1	6 000	1 200	4 800
2	4 800	960	3 840
3	3 840	768	3 072

Reducing balance (Computer)

Year	Book value at start	Depreciation	Book value at end
1	2 100	420	1 680
2	1 680	336	1 344
3	1 344	268.80	1 075.20
4	1 075.20	215.04	860.16
5	860.16	172.03	688.13

(1–8 marks)

(iii) *Application/Understanding*

- Both straight line and reducing balance are acceptable methods.
- The advantage of using reducing balance is that the amounts charged for depreciation in the earlier years are higher, and more representative of the true loss in value of vehicles and computers. **(1–2 marks)**

(c) *Knowledge*

- Depreciating fixed assets reduces their value in the books of a business.
- It also reduces the profits of the business, because depreciation is treated as an expense. **(1–4 marks)**

Application/Understanding

- Failure to depreciate fixed assets means that John will not be showing a 'true and fair view' of his fixed assets in the balance sheet.
- As a result, the fixed assets will be over valued and give a false impression of their worth.

Accounting and finance

- The yearly depreciation charge is also shown in the profit & loss account as a charge against gross profit: as a result, John's net profit will also be shown at too high an amount. **(5–8 marks)**

Analysis

- Too high a net profit will mean that John will pay more tax on his profits than necessary.
- When the assets are disposed of, the loss on their sale will be charged against profits, producing a substantially lower profit figure for the year in which the assets are sold. **(9–12 marks)**

Evaluation

- By not depreciating his fixed assets, John is also ignoring the accruals (matching) concept.
- This requires businesses to allocate expenses to the year or other period to which they refer.
- Dargon Distribution would not have its accounts accepted by the external auditors, and would therefore need to adjust for depreciation at some stage.
- Depreciation is an attempt to share the assets' cost across all the years for which the assets are held, and as a result it must be taken into account. **(13–18 marks)**

examiner's tip — You need to refer to the effect of depreciating assets in both the profit & loss account and the balance sheet. You should also mention the effect of non-depreciation when the fixed assets are eventually sold.

(2) (a) (i) *Knowledge*

- Relevant stakeholder groups include lenders and directors. **(1–2 marks)**

(ii) *Knowledge*

- Lenders are interested in a business's liquidity: its ability to meet their debts.
- They are also interested in its profitability: its ability to make sufficient profits, out of which loan interest and other payments to lenders can be made.
- Directors are interested in a company's efficiency, for example in collecting its debts.
- They are also interested in its profitability because the return they pay shareholders (dividend) is paid out of its taxed profits. **(1–3 marks)**

Application/Understanding

- MacLean plc is a public company so it will have directors.
- The directors of this plc will want to keep shareholders happy, for example by paying a healthy dividend on their shares.
- The dividend paid is £75 000, and in the year the company made an additional £120 000 that could also have been distributed as dividend.
- There is no sign of a debenture or other long-term loan in the balance sheet, but the plc does have a bank overdraft so the bank is a lender to this business.
- The bank has allowed an overdraft of £12 000, and will want to ensure MacLean plc can pay this back. **(4–8 marks)**

Analysis

- The plc's profitability record will influence shareholder views of the directors' performance.
- This will affect their likelihood of re-election.
- Directors may also receive performance-based pay, which is calculated on profit levels.
- Current assets are substantially above current liabilities, which suggests the bank may regard MacLean plc as being in a healthy liquidity position.
- However, most of the current assets are in the form of stocks, so MacLean will need to be able to sell these stocks in order to repay the bank's overdraft. **(9–12 marks)**

> **examiner's tip** There are a number of 'clues' in the final accounts figures. These figures should be included, described and analysed in your answer.

(b) *Knowledge* and *Application/Understanding*

- Gross profit % = 420/1120 = 37.5%
- Net profit % = 260/1120 = 23.2%
- Return on capital employed = 260/975 = 26.7%   **(1–8 marks)**

Analysis

- Compared with 2000, the gross profit margin has fallen from 40% to 37.5%.
- The net profit margin has also fallen, from 25% to 23.2% in 2001.
- ROCE has fallen from 30% in 2000 to 26.7% in 2001.
- Overall, there is a worse performance in 2001 in all three major profitability ratios. **(9–12 marks)**

Evaluation

- The fall in the gross profit margin of 2.5% should – other things being equal – lead to a similar-sized fall in the net profit margin.
- But this has only fallen by 1.8%, which means that MacLean plc has been more efficient in 2001 with its expenses (i.e., the difference between the two profit figures and profit margins).
- The fall in the ROCE could be due to a number of factors, such as expanding the company by investing in fixed assets.
- There may be a good reason for the falling profitability performance (e.g. expansion), but the directors will need to review this overall decline in profitability. **(13–18 marks)**

> **examiner's tip** Notice that the question asks you to evaluate **profitability** only, so there is no point in including (for example) ratios and comments about the company's liquidity.

(c) *Knowledge* and *Application/Understanding*

- Financial information is obtained from final accounts of a business such as MacLean plc, and can assess the profitability, liquidity and efficiency of such a company.
- Non-financial information is obtained from the performance of business functions, such as production, marketing and administration.
- The external environment within which a business such as MacLean plc operates is also relevant. **(1–8 marks)**

Analysis

- MacLean plc's additional financial information includes its share price and performance because it is a plc.
- Its past financial statements (profit and loss, balance sheet, cash flow statement) are also relevant because trends can be assessed from them.
- Non-financial information for MacLean plc includes internal issues such as staff morale, the quality and amount of staff recruitment and training, the extent to which its order book is full, its product portfolio and the position of these products in the product lifecycle, and the quality and age of its fixed assets.
- External factors include MacLean plc's market situation, and the actions of the government and its competitors. **(9–12 marks)**

Evaluation

- To make a full evaluation of MacLean plc's performance, both financial and non-financial factors need to be considered.
- Whilst the final accounts will show financial trends, any analysis is based on past financial information and is therefore of limited use only.
- There are still problems in assessing MacLean plc by examining relevant non-financial information, because it operates in a constantly changing environment that affects production, marketing and other functions.

(13–18 marks)

Chapter 6

Human resources management

Questions with model answers

Young enterprise becomes real

Sena Sikata and Richard Elliott had been the Joint Managing Directors of a Young Enterprise Company during their time at school five years ago. They had run a 'company' providing marketing services to local businesses. After leaving school they had decided to set up a 'real' company and chose to set up a business that provided administration services such as report binding and business stationery. It had proved to be fairly successful. However, although business was good and profits were high, they had always had problems with labour turnover, as shown by the following table.

Length of service	Number of employees
More than 1 year	2
6 months – 1 year	4
3 months – 6 months	4
Less than 3 months	6

(a) Outline what is meant by the phrase 'Labour Turnover'. [3]

(b) Calculate the Annual Labour Turnover implied by the table. [3]

(c) Evaluate how Sena and Richard might deal with the problems created by the high labour turnover. [15]

(d) Discuss the legal issues related to employment that Richard and Sena might need to consider when setting up a 'real' company. [10]

Examiner's Commentary

For help see Revise AS Study Guide pp. 93–94 and 98–100

55

C grade candidate – mark scored 15/31

(a) Labour turnover is the number of people who leave a company in a year.

(b) Turnover = 14

(c) The high labour turnover may be caused by the fact that the jobs are boring and badly paid. It may be that the workers who have been recruited in the past have been poorly chosen, so that they have not fitted in to the company or been unable to do the job very well. The workers may feel unappreciated and decide to go and work elsewhere.

The workers need to be better motivated. Maslow says that workers need to have their basic needs satisfied first, with a decent wage, but then want security needs and friendship needs. Maybe these are not being met. It is very unlikely that they will be able to obtain esteem and self-actualisation needs in this sort of job.

Taylor said that money was the only motivator. So maybe the workers should be paid more. Could they be given more responsibility or promotion to follow what Herzberg believed? Maybe the management style of Sena and Richard is not very good. They might be too autocratic or too laissez-faire. Sena and Richard should read about Douglas McGregor's X and Y theory. They certainly need to do something about the high labour turnover because it will be costing them money.

(d) There are lots of laws that will affect the business. For example, a fairly new law is the Working Time Regulations 1998, brought in as part of the UK's acceptance of The Social Charter. This means that all workers are entitled to four weeks' paid holiday a year, one day's rest a week and a maximum average of 48 hours work a week. The Health & Safety Act 1974 ensures that all employees are able to work in a safe working environment. Every employer must produce a written document about health and safety. Larger firms must have an accident book and a trained First Aider. If a company does not abide by the law they may be fined or taken to court.

The firm must also abide by The Disability Discrimination Act 1995, The Race Relations Act 1976 and The Sex Discrimination Act 1975. This means that Sena and Richard cannot refuse to employ someone because of the colour of their skin, their sex or a disability.

Other laws that must be followed are those that say all workers must have a written contract.

Examiner's Commentary

Labour turnover must be calculated relative to the size of the workforce. The number of people leaving Sainsburys in a year will be more than at the local bakers. But this does not mean that the baker's labour turnover is lower.

The question does not ask for the causes of the problem. They are worth mentioning briefly if you are then going to link them with how to resolve them. But this answer does not do that.

Why not?

This answer shows excellent knowledge of the relevant theory. It is a shame that it has not been better linked with the information about the company.

This is not a Law AS level. Detailed knowledge about dates and titles of the legislation is far less important than recognising how the law affects a business.

Not actually what the law says.

GRADE BOOSTER

A calculation question should always have the working shown in the answer.

A grade candidate – mark scored 29/31

(a) This is the rate at which employees leave a company, usually expressed as a percentage for the year. It can be calculated using the formula:

Labour Turnover

$= \dfrac{\text{Number of workers leaving a firm in one year}}{\text{Average number of staff employed in a year}} \times 100$

(b) Labour Turnover $= \dfrac{14}{16} \times 100$

$= 87.5\%$

If 14 employees have been with the company for less than one year it is fair to assume that they have replaced 14 workers who have left in the last year.

(c) With such a high labour turnover it would appear that this company has a serious problem with retaining its staff, although it would be useful to be able to compare this figure with the industry average. The nature of the job will be mainly unskilled, which is likely to attract younger workers, including students. These workers are generally more mobile and are likely to move on to better jobs after a while. The level of pay will obviously be important and so it would be beneficial for Sena and Richard to find out what the average wage is for this sort of work. If they find that they are paying below the average then they may have to consider raising the wage rate to bring it in line with similar work. This should not be too much of a problem given the fact we are told that they are very profitable.

Good context.

They should also consider non-financial motivational strategies. There will be little scope for promotion in such a small firm and they may need to consider theorists such as Herzberg and Maslow. They both suggested that needs other than money are important. Greater responsibility may be a motivator, as part of job enrichment. Again, it may be difficult to enrich the type of jobs done in this company. Maybe Sena and Richard should consider asking the workers for their views. Not only will it help them to find out the cause of the high labour turnover, but the consultation may in itself act as a motivator.

Good link between theory and practice.

Whatever the reason for the high labour turnover, it is important to deal with it. This is because it will be costing the company a lot of money in recruitment and training costs. Ultimately, any extra money spent trying to resolve this problem may be less than the costs incurred if labour turnover is not reduced.

Clear evaluation because the costs and benefits are weighed up.

Examiner's Commentary

For help see Revise AS Study Guide pp. 93–94 and 98–100

A grade continued

Examiner's Commentary

(d) When setting up a business for real a number of legal issues related to employment are relevant. They include contracts, equal opportunities and health & safety.

Any worker employed must have a contract, with written particulars given in writing, within three months of starting work. This must include things such as hours worked, holiday rights and wage rate. Since 1998 all workers must be paid at least the minimum wage, which is currently £3.70 if you are aged over 21 and £3.35 if aged between 18 and 21.

> The law relating to contract of employment is confusing. Any minor errors here are less important than the general level of understanding shown.

All firms must abide by equal opportunities legislation, which covers discrimination by sex, race or disability. For example, no job can be refused because of the colour of your skin or because you are a woman. However, this company will be exempt from the disability legislation because they employ fewer than 20 workers. This means that they can refuse to employ a disabled worker because of the extra costs and inconvenience that it will cause - although this may be seen as unethical.

> A good knowledge of the law shown, with wider issues identified.

All firms, regardless of their size, are responsible for ensuring the health and safety of their employees and third parties. Sena and Richard should ensure that training is provided for using dangerous equipment, such as binding machines. The company must produce a health and safety policy and carry out regular risk assessments to minimise the chance of accidents.

Failure to conform to these laws and others may lead to Sena and Richard being taken to court and/or fined, which will create bad publicity and make it even more difficult to recruit and retain good workers.

Exam practice questions

1

McDONALD'S

McDonald's, the fast food business, is regarded as a centralised organisation that makes decisions at the top. Centralised decisions include setting quality standards for supplies of raw materials as well as deciding on the layout and style of McDonald's restaurants. The larger outlets have a general manager. These large restaurants have the power to run their operations with less direction from head office. General managers can go on to become supervisors who look after a group of restaurants in a particular region.

Julie Room is the general manager of McDonald's, Festival Park in Stoke on Trent. The Festival Park restaurant serves around 16 000 customers each week and is open 7 am–midnight, seven days a week. The restaurant has 103 employees. Seventy per cent of the employees work on a part-time basis. One of Julie's responsibilities is to select, interview and appoint staff. 'We hire people on a regular basis: staff are always leaving and we need to employ new people continually.'

Julie says: 'Promotion prospects in McDonald's are very good. All the managers in this restaurant, and 80 per cent of McDonald's senior managers, started off as crew members'.

'Most of our training is on site and usually on the job training. We have a buddy system, so that when someone first starts they are paired with an experienced employee who is part of the training squad for 3 weeks. When new employees are considered competent to work in an area of the restaurant they are given a star.'

To get this star new employees have to pass tests. These consist of a verbal test and observation by their buddy. These observations are centred on a checklist, which consists of 20–25 procedures the employees should know about for each area. 'Employees need to get a 90 per cent pass mark in their unit test in order to achieve a star', explains Julie Room. 'It takes about a month to achieve a star and they find it quite motivating.

Source: adapted from S CURTIS, 'McDonald's Star Treatment', *Business Review*, September 1999

(a) (i) What is meant by the term 'on the job training' (line 17)? [2]

(ii) Briefly explain **two** reasons why training might be important to McDonald's. [4]

(b) With reference to motivation theory, outline **two** ways in which McDonald's attempts to motivate its employees. [6]

(c) Examine the factors that one of McDonald's general managers might need to take into account when planning for future workforce needs. [8]

(d) McDonald's operates a centralised organisational structure. To what extent might this prove beneficial to the company? [10]

[AQA, January 2001]

ALL CHANGE AT MIDSHIRE

The recent decline in profits at Midshire Confectionery has prompted a shake up at the Warwick-based chocolate manufacturer. The retirement of long-serving Managing Director Tom Marsh has created a move away from a paternalistic leadership style. Helen Williams has been appointed as the new Chief Executive along with three new directors. These changes are expected to result in a more democratic approach to leadership at Midshire. It is anticipated that the firm will introduce new methods of working for employees at all levels. For many years the company has had high labour costs and has made relatively little use of machinery on the production line. Productivity has been low and poor quality output has been a common problem.

A spokesperson outlined the extent of the changes at the company. 'The new management team intends to base the organisation around a much wider span of control, whilst implementing more capital-intensive production techniques. Midshire has a committed workforce, but one which has not been used effectively over recent years. Workers will be given more independence in their working lives, but more will be expected of them. It is vital that Midshire improves its competitiveness in international markets.'

The spokesperson continued: 'The new management team is seeking to create a very different organisation through the use of human resource management. The effective management of the labour force is seen as vital if the company is to prosper. Midshire expects to gain a number of benefits from introducing a policy of single status. Helen Williams is determined to make the workforce more productive. She believes leadership style is the most important influence on the performance of the workforce.'

It is expected that approximately 600 jobs will be lost as a result of these changes. The firm currently employs 2080 workers. Employees are very concerned that large numbers of redundancies may occur. Representatives from the workforce are expected to seek talks with the new management team.

(a) Explain what is meant by the following terms:

    (i) 'paternalistic leadership style' (line 3) [3]

    (ii) 'single status' (line 20) [3]

(b) Outline **two** benefits Midshire might expect as a result of adopting a more capital-intensive approach to production. [6]

(c) Midshire plans to introduce new methods of working that will place greater demands on its employees. Analyse possible ways in which human resource management might help the company to introduce these changes successfully. [8]

(d) Helen Williams, the new Chief Executive believes that 'leadership style is the most important influence on the performance of the workforce' (line 22). To what extent do you agree with her view? [10]

[AQA, June 2001]

examiner's tip — Each of these questions should be completed in about 35 minutes.

Answers

(1) (a) (i) *Knowledge*

A suitable definition would be 'Instruction at the place of work on how the job should be carried out'. This may include observing an experienced employee or being talked through the job by a supervisor. **(1–2 marks)**

(ii) *Knowledge*
- Improved customer service
- Increased employee morale/motivation
- Attract better employees
- Retain existing employees better **(1–2 marks)**

Understanding/Application

The benefits for McDonald's may include:
- Better customer service by employees that leads to happier customers.
- Better service by employees because they are more motivated/qualified.
- Training employees may help McDonald's to achieve its corporate objectives. **(3–4 marks)**

(b) *Knowledge*
- Promotion, recognition and achievement. There is also an attempt to achieve the higher order needs according to Maslow, namely belonging needs, esteem & ego needs and self-actualisation. **(1–2 marks)**

Understanding/Application
- Julie Room states that promotion prospects are very good and gives examples of managers who started as crew members.
- The efforts of crew members are rewarded by being given competence stars.
- By providing a buddy system the new employee quickly gets to know people in the workplace so helping them to build up friendships.
- Managers in the larger restaurants are able to satisfy self-actualisation needs because they have power to run their operations with less control from head office. **(3–6 marks)**

> **examiner's tip**: It is very important with questions about motivational theory that your answer does not become a repetition of all the theorists you can remember. You must apply the theory briefly to the case material.

(c) *Knowledge*
- Rate of labour turnover
- Expected demand for employees (based on demand for product)
- Changes in the skills required of the workforce
- Any changes in the working practices planned
- Changes in the area of employment law **(1–2 marks)**

Human resources management

Understanding/Application

Factors specific to McDonald's include:

- Changes in customer demand patterns, such as when are the busiest times of the day, will lead to a greater need for flexible working hours, so leading to more part-time workers.
- Increased labour turnover may mean that the general managers have to increase their employee advertising and training budget.
- Changes in employment law providing more flexible hours for workers with young children will lead managers to examine staffing rotas to prevent a lack of staff at certain times of the day. **(3–6 marks)**

Analysis

- Changes in working practices that lead to increased productivity will allow the general managers to reduce staffing levels. However, this may also reduce the level of flexibility that is needed in this type of business.
- More competition from other fast food outlets and a continuation of the recent negative publicity surrounding McDonald's will lead to general managers reducing employment levels. Alternatively, they may look for ways of winning back customers by employing more skilled employees to provide a better level of service. **(7–8 marks)**

(d) *Knowledge/Understanding*

Benefits include:

- Senior managers have more control of the business.
- Procedures such as purchasing can be centralised which leads to better economies of scale.
- Senior managers are possibly more skilled at making decisions of a better quality. **(1–2 marks)**

Analysis

- Although senior managers may be better at making the decisions, do they have the time to make all the decisions so reducing their effectiveness?
- Can senior managers at head office have the local knowledge that allows decisions to be made in a more relevant way for individual stores?
- The fact that all decisions are made centrally limits the experience being gained by individual general managers so limiting their experience when they become supervisors.
- Centralised decision-making is typically inflexible and bureaucratic and therefore not suitable for a dynamic market such as fast food. **(3–7 marks)**

examiner's tip Although this question may appear to be phrased as asking you about the benefits of centralisation this is not the case. The phrase 'to what extent' is a favourite one for examiners to use when asking candidates to discuss the advantages and disadvantages. In fact this discussion of both sides of the argument is the most efficient way to achieve Level 3 (analysis). To clearly show which side you agree with in the context of the question is what examiners are looking for to award Level 4 (evaluation).

Evaluation

The advantages and disadvantages need to be summed up with a judgement made. For example, although the centralisation of decisions may be quick, relatively cheap and allows head office to keep a firm control over the company's activities, the impact on local general managers may be demotivating, with many decisions being irrelevant to the local market. There is therefore a danger that customers feel alienated and the general feeling that McDonald's is too global to be relevant to local markets, is exacerbated. **(8–10 marks)**

> **examiner's tip** There is no right answer to this question. As long as you justify your argument, you may conclude that centralisation is either good or bad for McDonalds.

(2) (a) (i) *Knowledge*

When leaders take decisions in what they consider to be the best interests of their employees. Paternalistic leaders tend to explain their decisions to their subordinates, with communication being normally downward only.

(1–3 marks)

(ii) *Knowledge*

This is the removal of discrimination between different grades of employees within an organisation by providing the same facilities and benefits for all. For example, all employees use the same restaurant, car park and work the same hours and benefit from the same sick pay and holiday arrangements.

(1–3 marks)

(b) *Knowledge*

Benefits of a more capital-intensive approach to production include:

- Less reliance on expensive human resources
- Reduction in industrial relations problems
- More consistent quality levels
- Better levels of productivity. **(1–2 marks)**

Understanding/Application

- Given that we are told that Midshire Confectionery have had low productivity the introduction of more capital-intensive methods will increase efficiency and so reduce costs.
- Given the firm's stated wish to improve competitiveness in international markets, improved productivity, more consistent quality levels and the reduced threat of industrial relations problems will assist greatly. **(3–6 marks)**

(c) *Knowledge*

- Workforce planning is a central part of HRM and will allow the company to assess its likely labour needs in the future.
- It compares the future human needs with the current labour supply, indicating likely surpluses and shortages. **(1–2 marks)**

Understanding/Application
- Increased independence for the employees will require training of the workforce to prepare them for their more empowered role.
- A wider span of control mentioned in line 11 will also change the daily working life of managers. It is also HRM's responsibility to train and prepare managers for these fairly considerable transformations to their working life. **(3–5 marks)**

> **examiner's tip** The application of pure knowledge to specific situations in the case material is the way to ensure that the examiner rewards you at this level.

Analysis
- Even though the HRM department is trying to prepare employees for the proposed changes there may still be problems. The fact that 600 jobs (nearly a third of the workforce) are under threat may mean that workers are more concerned about this than co-operating willingly with any training or development provided by the HRM department.
- There may also be resistance because of the culture of the company developed during the long period operating under a paternalistic leader. It will take time for workers to come to terms, without being suspicious, of the intentions of the new Chief Executive. **(6–8 marks)**

(d) *Knowledge/Understanding*
- Leaders set objectives and standards for the organisation and employees so they do have an important influence.
- Successful leadership can be very motivating for employees at all levels.
(1–2 marks)

Analysis
There are however, other equally important factors, including:
- The level of training and skill level of the employees is a major determinant of worker performance. If the workers cannot do the job very well then even the best leader will find it difficult to improve the performance of staff.
- Lack of suitable capital equipment will seriously hinder the performance. This firm will find it difficult to increase productivity without the introduction of more and/or better machinery.
- Most motivational theorists suggest that pay and other financial benefits are significant factors. Herzberg in particular says that if the basic 'Hygiene factors' such as pay are absent then the 'Motivators' such as good leadership cannot have any influence. **(3–7 marks)**

Evaluation
Evaluation may focus on the thought that leadership is more important in times of crisis, when profit margins are slim, or at a time of significant change, as in the case of Midshire Confectionery. On the other hand, businesses with strong brands and skilled, highly motivated employees are less likely to be dependent upon effective leadership. **(8–10 marks)**

Chapter 7 — Marketing

Questions with model answers

Business on the Internet

Valerie Fulton, of NTL, reveals how the Internet can draw a host of new admirers to your business.

How can I put my business on the Internet?

There are many talented website designers available locally who will design your site for you. Prices range from around £50 per page.

You then need to get the newly designed site onto the web and you can expect to pay at least £100 for set-up with a running cost of at least £50 per year.

How do I let people know about my new website?

Many companies, including some of the best known in the world, have adapted their traditional newspaper and magazine advertising to direct customers to their web sites. All you have to do to promote your website address is to add it to the bottom of adverts in the same way as you would use your phone number or mailing address. You can also add it to your stationery.

You have mentioned e-mail as a way of customers communicating with my business but I'd prefer to talk directly to anyone who has visited my website. What's your advice?

The simplest solution is to provide a freephone number on your website, that means that people who are interested will be able to phone you at no cost to themselves. Your website and freephone number also have the advantage of allowing you to promote a 'national image' for your business even if you are working from a small office in a small town in Northern Ireland. One company I know of has had 2186 freephone calls as a result of its website in just three months.

I'm tired of hearing about the need to put my business on the World Wide Web. What makes you think I need to do this?

The actual numbers of firms going onto the web and doing business is definitely growing. There are plenty of well-documented surveys from respected independent research companies. Anyone, anywhere in the world, can find out about your business. This is the marketing method of the future!

Source: adapted from *The Business Telegraph* 17 August, 1999 and 14 September, 1999

(a) Explain how a website and freephone number have the advantage of allowing a firm to promote a 'national image' even if it is run from a small office in a small town in Northern Ireland. [6]

(b) Discuss the impact that a new website may have on the traditional methods of promoting a business. [10]

(c) Evaluate the use of the Internet as a tool for mass marketing. [14]

[CCEA, Specimen]

Examiner's Commentary

For help see Revise AS Study Guide pp. 106–117

Most marks in (a) appear to be for levels 1 (Knowledge) and 2 (Application). When answering (b), you need to make analytical points to obtain most of these marks. Part (c) asks for a Level 4 response.

C grade candidate – mark scored 15/30

Examiner's Commentary

(a) A website will have its own 'www' address, which could be anywhere in the country, and so it could easily be taken as a national company. The offer of a freephone number is also associated with larger, nationally-based companies.

The candidate hasn't really explained how freephone numbers might be used.

(b) Businesses tend to use a combination of traditional advertising media such as TV, radio, newspapers and billboards, but this will depend on what is being sold and promoted. More and more people now have access to the Internet: as a result, businesses are creating their own websites to promote themselves and their products. This can be an efficient way of doing this, since it is low in cost and the website can be easy to maintain once it has been set up. Some businesses now rely largely on their websites to sell their products or services, such as the 'dot.com' companies based on the Internet. They tend not to use the traditional methods of promotion. Those businesses that do will have to reallocate some of their resources to Internet promotion.

Although there are some well-explained points, the answer lacks detail, and some of it is not related fully to the question asked.

(c) I would recommend the use of an Internet website for any business. It brings a range of advantages, with hardly any drawbacks. Although there will be an initial cost in setting up the website the business will find that it will get many 'hits', perhaps even thousands, which will alert Internet users to the business and what it has to offer. The advantages of the website are that it remains there even when the business premises are closed, so a customer can get in touch (using e-mail) at any time, day or night. This also allows the business to contact its customers through e-mail. Since prospective customers in other countries can also find the business website, sales are bound to increase.

An over-optimistic answer, which fails to analyse the limitations of websites. The answer would also be strengthened by comparing and contrasting with other tools for mass marketing.

GRADE BOOSTER

A stronger answer would explain how different businesses use different methods of promotion in **(b)**, and the problems people may have in finding a business website in **(c)**.

A grade candidate – mark scored 27/30

Examiner's Commentary

(a) The information on the website will be under the control of the owners, and the firm's address need not feature. There is also no way to tell where a firm is located from a freephone number. The firm can therefore project a national image. The quality of the website and the way the freephone responses are handled are also factors in projecting an image: a small firm can therefore create a professional image more associated with large companies.

> Some clear points made here, though perhaps a real-life example would further strengthen the answer.

> For help see Revise AS Study Guide pp. 106–117

(b) The traditional methods of promoting products are being threatened through more frequent use of the Internet by people, as computers, mobile phones and other technological developments (e.g. TV shopping) lead towards greater Internet access. One important factor is that, since there will be a limited budget for advertising and promotion, more and more of this budget may be being spent on the firm's website: as a result there will be less finance available for the more traditional promotional methods. These promotional methods will also be affected by the new website: for example, advertisements in papers and on radio will carry the firm's website address, encouraging people to access it. More and more firms are using their websites not only to gain hits from potential customers, but also as a two-way medium, e.g. by allowing these customers to download catalogues, order forms, and other materials. This can result in substantial cost savings for the firm (e.g. printing costs are borne by the customer, and less storage space is required by the firm).

> This is a good illustration of how to 'discuss', because a balanced answer has been presented.

> Stronger answers won't be limited to marketing only, but will draw on other areas such as finance.

The business can also promote its image and mission through its website. The 'virtual' business can be seen through pictures and video clips, and the image can be enhanced through professional presentation. This compares well with the traditional methods of using brochures, and is very cost-effective when compared to the expense of corporate advertising through television or national newspapers. The website must remain up-to-date, however, in order to promote a professional image.

> The question asks about 'promoting a business', not just its products, which is recognised in this answer.

(c) Because the Internet is a global medium of communication, it has great value as a tool for mass marketing. Anyone with Internet access can access a firm's website from anywhere in the world. It is also relatively inexpensive to establish an Internet presence, and British firms are fortunate in that English is the dominant Internet language. This is of tremendous benefit to many small firms that could only otherwise afford to promote on a small-scale (even local) basis. The Internet site can be accessed 24 hours a day, every day, when the firm is otherwise 'closed'. It also lets a two-way dialogue take place: the company can allow access to materials such as downloadable brochures, and can set up ordering systems (e.g. using e-mail). In conclusion, the website compares favourably with many of the other, traditional, methods of mass promotion, on grounds of cost and accessibility.

> This is a good analysis of the main issues in favour of Internet use, with the candidate giving clear reasons to support the points made.

Marketing

67

A grade continued

However, the website will need substantial promotion, especially in its early days. Internet access in many countries is restricted, either by attempted government interference, or more commonly by the cost and availability of the required equipment. Computer skills are also needed in order to access the Internet. Furthermore, it is not always easy, given the millions of pages available, for an individual firm to make its presence felt on the Internet: it will need to rely on efficient searching by the user, unless it can otherwise communicate its address (which will require the use of another medium, e.g. newspaper adverts featuring its website address). This searching is also likely to produce the websites of competitors, which may affect the firm's sales. Finally, the Internet site will need to be regularly monitored and controlled, to ensure that it remains up-to-date and relevant for the firm's customers, so there will be a continuing cost associated with its existence.

Examiner's Commentary

There is evidence of evaluation here. The candidate has now balanced this answer by explaining and analysing some key problems of Internet/website use. Perhaps a more detailed conclusion might have been included, e.g. by reaching a judgement in favour of using the Internet in marketing.

Exam practice questions

1 Read the following passage and then answer the questions that follow.

BOOTS CARD TOPS TEN MILLION MARK

Boots the Chemist will have ten million Advantage Cardholders by Christmas 1999, two million more than originally anticipated. The new figures also reveal that 95% of the cardholders are female.

The company claims the card has been successful because of its unique emotional positioning, which encourages customers to treat themselves to products using their loyalty points.

'The Advantage Card is our most important marketing tool and we have ambitious plans as to how we are going to use it next year,' said Crawford Davidson, Boots Advantage Card marketing group manager. This includes more segmented mailing according to lifestyle, level of loyalty and a prediction of types of products purchased, as well as changes to categories and store positioning.

Card data showed that new mothers buy more photographic material. Store planning and promotions around the traditionally male-interest category were given a more female focus.

(a) Explain **two** reasons why so many large retail businesses have introduced loyalty cards. [4]

(b) Discuss the view that the loyalty cards are ineffective unless all of the other necessary marketing elements are in place. [6]

(c) Analyse both the costs and benefits to Boots of placing greater emphasis on segmentation in its marketing policy. [8]

[WJEC, 2000]

2 Study the information and answer **all** parts of the question that follows.

THE BEST THING SINCE SLICED BREAD

British Bakeries has taken the decision to update Hovis, one of Britain's best-known products. Hovis is a brown, wholemeal loaf. Substantial market research had shown British Bakeries that its products and advertising were out of touch with modern families. Also the market for bread has changed. White bread has increased in popularity over the last ten years. In 1985 wholemeal bread held 17% of the market, but by 1995 its market share had fallen to 12%. British Bakeries is a subsidiary of the giant food manufacturer RHM and competes with other large firms in a mass market.

British Bakeries has launched a new loaf, using the Hovis name, designed to please the entire family. *Best of Both* has a unique selling point as it contains enough fibre and wheat germ to be classified as brown bread, but has the look, taste and texture of white bread. Simultaneously, the company's advertising has changed dramatically: *Best of Both* appears in adverts featuring cartoon characters that would not look out of place in South Park or The Simpsons. Animated adverts are accompanied by eye-catching new packaging.

Developing and launching the new product has required a huge investment by British Bakeries. *Best of Both* is still at the introductory stage of its product life cycle and its sales figures are being watched closely. However, the company is confident that the loaf will be a financial success.

Best of Both is the result of carefully planned primary market research. The company conducted qualitative market research revealing that women favour brown bread for healthy reasons, but children and men prefer white bread. British Bakeries' product was tested by focus groups of families and children; pupils in a London school were asked to try *Best of Both* for breakfast.

Nutritionists are sceptical about the health benefits of a white loaf, even if it is classified as brown. A spokesperson commented that most of the health benefits of brown bread come from husks of wheat, which have been removed from *Best of Both*. Competitors have been impressed however, and one of them, Kingsmill, is to launch a rival product.

(a) Explain what is meant by the following terms:

    (i) 'primary market research' (line 19); [3]

    (ii) 'qualitative market research' (line 20). [3]

(b) *Best of Both* is in the introductory stage of its product life cycle. Outline **two** possible financial implications of this for British Bakeries. [6]

(c) *Best of Both* has a unique selling point (USP). Examine **two** benefits British Bakeries might receive from this USP. [8]

(d) British Bakeries carried out extensive market research before introducing *Best of Both* onto the market. To what extent might this make sure that this new product succeeds? [10]

[AQA, Summer 2002]

Answers

(1) (a) *Knowledge*
- Loyalty cards allow segmentation to take place and provide Boots and other large retailers with information about their customers' shopping and buying habits.
- As a result, such retailers can target their markets much more effectively.
- The cards are a type of non-price competition: loyalty is created and repeat purchases encouraged, which benefits the retailer through retaining rather than losing the consumer. **(1–4 marks)**

> **examiner's tip**: Two reasons are asked for: for each, the marks are likely to be (1) for a basic statement plus (1) for expansion.

(b) *Knowledge*
- The above answer suggests that the loyalty card can play an important role in overall marketing strategy.
- It encourages repeat purchases, and provides the retailer with information that would otherwise not be available. **(1–2 marks)**

Application/Understanding
- As a result, retailers can plan their marketing strategies more effectively. **(3 marks)**

Analysis
- On its own, however, it is less effective than if it is used with other marketing ploys.
- Examples from the marketing mix include promoting the card itself, and linking additional special offers with card purchases.
- There must also be a satisfactory overall 'mix' for the card to be effective: e.g. suitable pricing policies, appropriate advertising and promotion, acceptable locations, and products that appeal to consumers.
- The loyalty card will support this mix, but is of little use without it. **(4–6 marks)**

> **examiner's tip**: Notice how a conclusion is reached, based on the points made in the answer. This approach may be valuable when you are asked to 'discuss' something.

(c) *Knowledge*

'Market segmentation' involves breaking the market into its constituent elements, e.g. on the basis of age, sex or other relevant characteristic. **(1–2 marks)**

Application/Understanding
- An example is the existence of 'niche' markets, which appeal to and supply a single market segment.
- As a result of segmentation, Boots can target different groups who have similar needs, and develop and promote products focused on these different groups. **(3–4 marks)**

Analysis
- Segmentation also encourages a policy of diversification, which is a safer policy for a firm than over-reliance on a single mass-market product.
- One drawback of segmentation is that it may be more difficult to produce a standardised product for the mass market: the firm may therefore lose the opportunity of economies of scale.
- However, mass market products will not appeal to everyone in the mass market, which is an argument in favour of segmentation policies. **(5–8 marks)**

> **examiner's tip** It is often valuable to briefly define or describe a key term such as 'segmentation'. However, the answer must concentrate on costs and benefits 'to Boots': points made must be relevant to this retailer and its market (for example, the reference to 'mass marketing').

(2) (a) *Knowledge*

(i) Primary market research is when information is collected for the first time, e.g. by using street interviews. This information is collected for a specific purpose. **(3 marks)**

(ii) Qualitative market research involves obtaining personal views of consumers about factors that motivate them to buy certain products. It is often obtained by interviewing small (focus) groups. **(3 marks)**

> **examiner's tip** You don't have to relate these terms to Hovis or British Bakeries, so only give general definitions.

(b) *Knowledge*
- A new product requires British Bakeries to invest heavily in promoting it.
- The introduction of Kingsmill's competing product might lead British Bakeries to cut the price of *Best of Both*. **(1–2 marks)**

Application/Understanding
- A major promotion campaign will mean large cash outflows on (e.g.) television advertising to create product awareness.
- If British Bakeries decides to cut the price of *Best of Both*, this will affect its sales revenue. **(3–4 marks)**

> **examiner's tip** The answer needs to consider both marketing and financial issues to receive full marks.

(c) *Knowledge*
- USP allows a business to differentiate its product from those of its competitors. **(1–2 marks)**

Application
- British Bakeries can use the USP to differentiate its bread from competing bakeries.
- It can also use the USP when promoting the bread, and to charge a premium price for it. **(3–4 marks)**

Analysis
- There is evidence in the context that sales for brown bread are falling, and so the existence of a USP with this 'brown' bread may help British Bakeries to maintain sales in a market with falling demand.
- The focus on healthy eating may allow British Bakeries to meet the needs of the whole family, encouraging more men and children to take up brown bread. **(5–8 marks)**

> **examiner's tip** The context must be used effectively to reach the expected Level 3 (Analysis) answer.

(d) *Knowledge*
- Market research is the process of examining the nature of the firm's market. **(1–2 marks)**

Application/Understanding
- There is evidence that British Bakeries has considered the views of consumers (focus groups tasting the prototype product, health aspects of brown bread being recognised, accounting for the differing tastes of men/children and women), which is a major feature in market research. **(3–4 marks)**

Analysis
- The use of market research will help British Bakeries to set a suitable price for the new bread.
- As a result of this market research, the marketing mix for *Best of Both* is likely to be appropriate for the product and its market.
- However, there is evidence that promotion of the product has alerted certain groups to be critical of the health claims, and a rival (Kingsmill) has already reacted to the introduction of this new product. **(5–7 marks)**

Evaluation
- Although market research will provide relevant information such as that explained above, it cannot account fully for possible reactions of competitors and other stakeholders.
- There is also no guarantee of the quality of any market research.
- As a result, British Bakeries may have to modify its marketing strategy. **(8–10 marks)**

> **examiner's tip** Make sure that you keep referring to the company and the product, and base your evaluation on sound analysis of the situation.

Chapter 8: Productive efficiency

Questions with model answers

C grade candidate – mark scored 6/14

VERTIGO ROCK Ltd

Helen and Jenny Saunders have been running a small family company, making seaside rock and other confectionery novelties for the last 12 years. They have recently moved to a new industrial unit based in Eastbourne. The products they manufacture are traditional sticks of rock, in a range of different colours and flavours. This is fairly profitable, although the seasonal nature of the product does cause a number of production and financial problems.

The high demand in the summer months is not a problem, as they begin production soon after Christmas and build up stocks steadily. This is necessary as rock is best produced in small batches. The real problem is keeping their workers busy and funds coming in between October and March when not much rock is sold.

(a) Explain the meaning of batch production. [4]

(b) Helen has suggested that the company produce a range of Christmas rock novelties. Discuss the implications for production of this proposal. [10]

For help see Revise AS Study Guide pp. 120 & 124

Examiner's Commentary

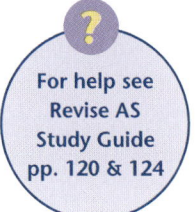

(a) The production of products in batches. The economic batch quantity can be calculated using a formula containing set-up costs, demand and holding costs.

> This student has not defined the term. It is best to avoid using the word being defined in your definition. The answer gains one mark for evidence of some relevant knowledge about how the batch level can be calculated.

(b) The batch production method currently being used by Vertigo can be used for the production of Christmas rock novelties. They will probably be able to use the same machinery, although the workers may need extra training to teach them to make the new products. This training may be on-the-job or off-the-job. Vertigo will probably not be able to afford to provide much training so they will have to do it themselves.

The main problem with batch production is that time is lost having to change the equipment to produce different products. If they are now making different rock novelties they may find that their costs go up because they spend so much time resetting the equipment.

> Although this student seems to know quite a bit about the method of production being used, the answer has two main faults. First, the sentences about the different types of training are not really relevant to the question and cannot therefore gain any marks. Second, there is poor use of the case material and so no real analysis can take place. Compare this with the answer by the student who gained an A grade.

GRADE BOOSTER

Even when the case material is short there should be some evidence that can be used.

A grade candidate – mark scored 13/14

Examiner's Commentary

(a) This is when a limited number of products are made in one go, where the whole batch passes through one stage of production before moving on to the next. This method is best used when the products are identical, except for one or two small changes. For example, the sticks of rock are identical, except for the flavouring and colouring, which can be added to each batch as needed.

The student has produced a clear definition and used the case material to provide an example.

(b) Helen's suggestion would help to fill the gap in the company's production run and provide very welcome extra finance. However, there are a number of issues that they must consider before going ahead with the idea.

They need to be sure that there is a suitable market demand for the product and that the extra revenue gained will exceed the additional costs incurred. Will new machinery be needed? Will the staff need retraining? The fact that they have just moved to new premises may mean there is sufficient space for expansion, although it may also mean that they are still coming to terms with the new facilities and will not really want the added pressure caused by producing a new product.

A good answer needs to recognise that there are going to be some problems with any proposal.

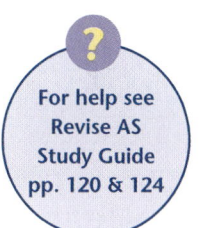

Ultimately, the fact that they have adequate spare capacity because of the seasonal nature of the rock, and that the novelties are basically the same product should mean that any additional costs for machinery and training are minimal. However, the potential benefits are great if it means that workers are kept busy. Productivity is therefore improved and a more regular source of cash is achieved.

For help see Revise AS Study Guide pp. 120 & 124

Exam practice questions

1 Barstow Engineering manufactures electrical motors sold to firms making washing machines and refrigerators. Production is organised into teams of workers each with a production supervisor. Any order is treated as a single batch and is allocated to a team, which is then responsible for its completion.

There has been heavy investment lately in production technology, thus creating flexibility and allowing teams to switch between products quickly. Since these changes, Barstow has become concerned about unreliable delivery of components by its supplier. Barstow's stock control chart for a particular component for the period January–May 1999 is shown in Figure 1. Quality control was not considered important, given the new machinery. Checking is now left to the supervisor. Labour turnover has increased over the past two years as the younger workers have left to join firms which offer training schemes. Recently, there have been a disturbing number of complaints about falling product standards and an increase in the number of rejected products returned by customers. One major customer has threatened to buy from a rival company if Barstow cannot produce a 'quality product'.

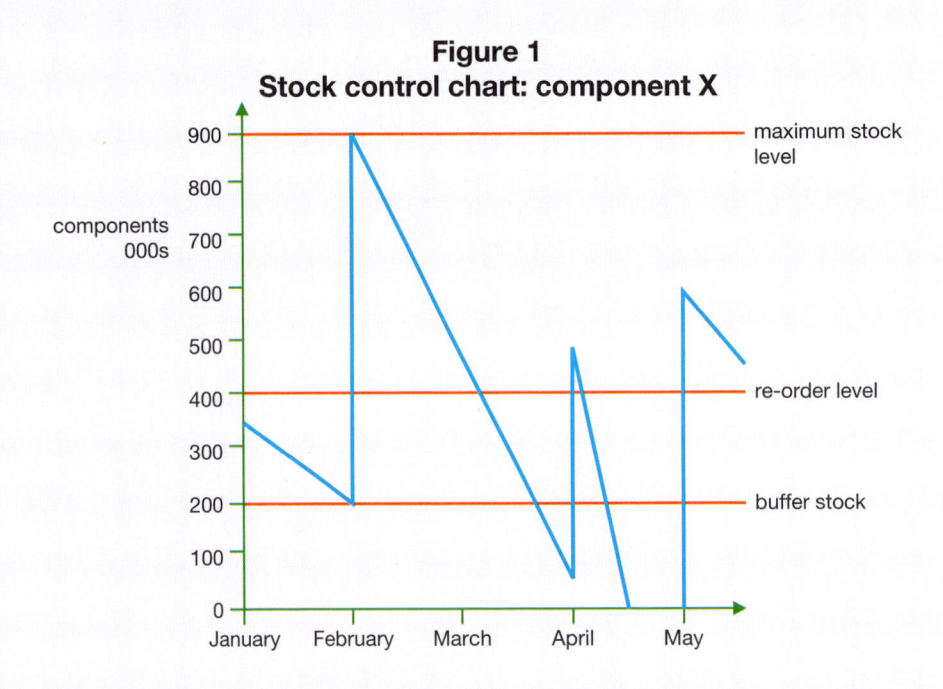

**Figure 1
Stock control chart: component X**

(stock control chart showing components 000s on y-axis from 0 to 900, months January to May on x-axis; maximum stock level at 900, re-order level at 400, buffer stock at 200)

(a) (i) Explain and comment upon the term 'buffer stock' as used in Figure 1. [4]

(ii) Calculate the average monthly usage of component X. [4]

(iii) Define 'lead time' and calculate it for the April delivery of component X. [4]

(b) One supervisor has suggested that the investment in new production technology might have led to the recent complaints from customers. Discuss ways in which the situation might be improved. [15]

[OCR AS Specimen Paper – Business Decisions (Question 2)]

> **examiner's tip** This question makes up one half of an AS module paper and therefore needs to be completed in no more than 35 minutes.

Answers on pages 78–80 Answers on pages 78–80 Answers on pages 78–80

2 The Ceramics Collection Ltd (CCL) was created in 1995 by four friends trying to earn a living from their pottery. As its markets have altered, the company has had to become much more *customer oriented*. This has led to some changes in production methods. Hand made items for local craft shops are still usually made to order. However the greater part of the revenue earned by the firm comes from a range of crockery that is sold through a chain of local department stores. These items are made by a batch production process using moulds. The business currently operates at 80 per cent capacity.

CCL has recently been approached by a potential new customer. This major high street retailer is interested in working with CCL to design and produce a new range of crockery. It will be sold exclusively under the retailer's brand name. The Production Director has some worries about the order and has raised these concerns in a memo to the Sales Director. See Fig. 1 below:

Memo

TO: Sales Director
FROM: Production Director
DATE: 10/5/02
SUBJECT: Special Crockery Order – Data

The initial order will be for 1200 crockery sets. Each set is made up of four items – one large and one small plate, a bowl and a mug. The retailer will pay us £12.00 per set. Further orders will depend on how successful sales are. However, output will have to increase by 30% if we are to take on this contract. I have worked out the direct costs as below:

Forecasted Direct Costs Per Item

	Large Plate	Small Plate	Bowl	Mug
Materials	£2.00	£1.50	£1.50	£2.00
Labour	£0.50	£0.50	£0.50	£1.00

The cost of purchasing the special machinery and moulds which are needed for this particular order will come to £2500.

I am worried about the potential problems arising from the required increase in capacity. We need a meeting with the Managing Director to discuss the implications of these figures.

(a) Briefly explain **two** problems that might arise for CCL from using batch production methods. [4]

(b) (i) Calculate the total contribution for accepting the high street retailer's order, stating any assumption that you make. [6]

(ii) Considering all aspects of the business, evaluate whether CCL should accept this new contract. [15]

[OCR – Module 2872, May 2002, Questions 1 (b) & (c)]

Answers

(1) (a) (i) *Knowledge*
Buffer stock is the minimum stock level. A company does not wish its stock level to fall below this point. **(1–2 marks)**

Understanding/Application
Barstow Engineering have a buffer stock level of 200 000 units. May need to be reassessed given the stock out that happened at the end of April. **(3–4 marks)**

examiner's tip
The three figures are found by calculating the size of orders in February, April and May.

(ii) Total Purchased = 700 000
400 000
600 000 +
1 700 000   **(1 mark)**

Stock Level Increase = Opening Stock − Closing Stock
= 450 000
350 000 −
= 100 000   **(1 mark)**

Total Sales = 1 700 000
100 000 −
1 600 000   **(1 mark)**

Average Monthly Sales = 1 600 000/5 = **320 000**   **(1 mark)**

examiner's tip
It is always a good idea to show as many stages of the working as possible. This helps you to work logically and helps the examiner to see how you got to the answer.

(iii) *Knowledge*
The lead time is the time taken between re-ordering the component from the supplier and the time when the new stock is received. **(1–2 marks)**

Understanding/Application
The stock received in April was ordered in March, so the lead time is one month. **(3–4 marks)**

examiner's tip
The lead time can be easily identified by following the stock level line back from the month when the stock arrives to the point where the line passes through the re-order level indicated by the horizontal line.

(b) *Knowledge*
- Introduce better training or TQM
- Introduce quality assurance rather than quality control
- Empower the workers
- Obtain customer feedback to identify the cause.   **(1–2 marks)**

Understanding/Application
- Workers are struggling with the change taking place and so need more training. There is evidence of insufficient training as 'younger workers have left to join firms which offer training schemes'.
- Given the move to a more empowered workforce it would make sense to give employees ownership of quality checking. This is a more efficient system than having a supervisor do it.   **(3–5 marks)**

Analysis

This may be shown by linking the possible cause with the appropriate effect. For example:

- The new investment in production technology will almost certainly have led to a change in method. Processes are likely to have become more mechanised and involve the use of CAM. Established workers may have resented this change and have regarded it as de-skilling, also with the removal of their opportunity for advancement within the organisation.

- Because the changes have been introduced without proper training, workers are struggling to cope with the change and possibly even the supervisors are not fully familiar with the new technology. Therefore, even when small flaws are noticed, this lack of familiarity makes all workers less keen to make adjustments.

- Empowering the workforce to exercise quality control functions by continuous checking of their own work should be easy to impose given the fact that they already work in production teams. **(6–9 marks)**

Evaluation

- The apparent increase in de-skilling of the workforce may be compensated by the increased recognition and responsibility provided by empowerment of the workers.

- The short-run problems, such as increased production technology, rapid change and increased flexibility should be outweighed by the long-run benefits of increased efficiency, lower costs and greater competitiveness.

(10–15 marks)

(2) (a) *Knowledge*

- Increased need for division of labour
- Unit costs may increase
- Machinery needs to be reset more often
- Increased work-in-progress. **(1–2 marks)**

Understanding/Application

Any problems mentioned need explaining briefly and in context for CCL. For example:

- The increased division of labour may make the jobs more repetitive and boring, which may affect motivation.

- The regular resetting of machinery will slow down production so increasing unit costs.

- Greater work-in-progress will increase costs and reduce cash flow. **(3–4 marks)**

(b) (i)

Total Revenue = 1200 sets × £12.00	= £14 400	(1 mark)
Direct Materials = 1200 sets × £7.00 = £8 400		(1 mark)
Direct Labour = 1200 sets × £2.50 = £3 000		(1 mark)
Total Direct Costs	= £11 400	
Contribution	= £3 000	(1 mark)
Less set-up costs	= £2 500	
Contribution for whole order	= £500	(1 mark)

Productive efficiency

Assumptions may include:
- The forecasts are accurate
- Price and direct costs remain constant
- The order cannot be taken without the set-up costs. **(1 mark)**

> **examiner's tip**
> If a question asks you to state an assumption then it is likely to be impossible to get full marks without thinking of at least one.

(ii) *Knowledge*

Identification of factors that might affect the decision to accept a contract, including:
- Physical capacity – is there any spare?
- Does the firm have enough staff?
- How will it be financed? **(1–2 marks)**

Understanding/Application
- This new contract only provides an extra £500 of contribution. Is it worth spending £2500 for such a small benefit?
- Could CCL's spare 20% capacity be used for a better offer in the future?
- Will methods of production be affected by this extra order?
- Extra staffing, if needed, will add to the costs of taking on this contract. **(3–5 marks)**

Analysis
- Although the contribution from this order appears relatively small it may be that this order leads to further larger and/or regular orders in the future. The customer is said to be a major high street retailer and so it would be safe to assume that potentially this could lead to a long-term and therefore highly profitable deal. In addition, any future orders will have a greater contribution as the £2500 cost of special machinery moulds is a one-off.
- There may be some concerns about taking on an order that leads to an increase in output of 30% when CCL only has 20% spare capacity. If this means that more staff need to be employed will they be able to recruit suitable staff? Will this lead to higher direct labour costs, so further reducing the contribution? Will there be issues related to managing greater numbers of staff?
- Will CCL benefit from economies of scale? As output increases they may expect average costs to fall so any contribution will be higher than expected. **(6–9 marks)**

Evaluation

A clear decision needs to be made, based on the evidence that has been already analysed. This may be along the lines of: Can CCL afford not to accept this order? It may be costly and present organisational problems in the short-run but the potential benefits of such a regular order from such a highly sought-after buyer are huge in the long-run.

However, an argument against the acceptance of this order may be that it has the potential to cause greater problems. CCL already have regular business with 'a chain of local department stores'. If this new contract puts that business in jeopardy will CCL end up being over reliant on this new customer? The problem with larger retailers is that they are always looking for cost advantages and are less likely to remain loyal to CCL. **(10–15 marks)**

> **examiner's tip**
> In questions that have a numerate part followed by a discursive part it is expected that candidates will use any data gained from the calculation to act as evidence in the later discussion.

AS Mock Exam 1

Centre number
Candidate number
Surname and initials

Letts

Business Studies

Time: 1 hour   Maximum marks: 45

Objectives and External Environment

Read the following extract then answer the questions which are based upon it.

Grading
Boundary for A grade   33/45
Boundary for C grade   27/45

JAM AT JAMES'

James Porter was made redundant, aged 35, in March 2002 and decided with his redundancy payment to start his own business. Playing guitar was something that had been his hobby since his teenage years and he had often wondered whether he would ever have the nerve to start up a music shop specialising in guitars and amplifiers.

He knew from experience that the town lacked a specialist music shop and all of the musicians he talked to were very enthusiastic. As a result of this encouragement he made a rough estimate of customer numbers, then he considered the factors likely to affect his ability to supply products to his customers. Finally he decided it would be worth taking the risk.

James knew that it was necessary to draw up a business plan and also to set clear objectives if he wanted to succeed. He thought that, with luck, he could make sufficient money to retire in about 20 years time. He saw endless possibilities in the range of equipment that he could eventually offer. He would start as a sole trader, he told himself, but he was sure that the business would grow quickly.

He used the Business Start Up pack from his bank as the basis for his plan. He found it quite straightforward and was able to obtain a loan of £25 000. This loan, along with his redundancy money, provided sufficient finance to buy the fixtures and stock for the new shop. *Jam at James'* opened for business in a rented unit at the start of May 2002. He had two part-time casual 'employees' (who were musician friends of his) to help out who he paid 'cash-in-hand'.

As his friends had predicted, there was a great deal of interest in the new shop – at least to start with. James kept a rough record of the number of visitors to the shop each month by keeping a tally on a sheet of paper (Table 1) whenever he remembered. By mid-October he was wondering whether he might expand his business by renting the unit next door. This had been a fish and chip shop that had closed the previous year. Perhaps it could be used as a rehearsal area for bands. He thought it would cost about £4000 to convert.

However, by early February 2003 these ideas had been completely disregarded. James' trade had slowed considerably and the future did not look as promising as it had only a few months ago. He now had only one person helping him out in the shop – and that was only for a few hours a day. Running a business in practice was not as easy as it had seemed on paper, he thought sadly. At first when trade had slowed down, he had simply used the time to practise on his guitar but, he now had to admit to himself, the lack of anything to do during the day was making his life rather boring. He wondered whether, taking the good months with the bad, he had actually made a success of his first year's trading. He was 'his own boss', he reflected, but he certainly had less money to spend than when he was an employee.

One morning in early April, James was staring gloomily at some particularly expensive guitars. He was managing to pay the rent on the unit but was wondering how long he would be able to keep up the interest payments on his loan. He had not liked what he had read in his newspaper that morning (Appendix 1). At that moment someone he had met at a concert a few months ago, and whom he vaguely remembered as being called Andy, walked in.

'Hi Mate,' said Andy. 'It's about time I called in on you. How's it going? Why are you looking so down? I thought you said things were really good.'

James explained why he was feeling worried about the state of the business.

'I may be able to help.' replied Andy. 'I've got a few electric guitar leads, well about two hundred, that you could have cheap.'

James asked how much they would cost and where Andy had got them from.

'I got them … er … from a mate who got them from … um er … a factory in Eastern Europe I think it was, that closed down. The quality isn't brilliant and they probably won't last as long as your usual ones but beginners won't notice! You can have them for two quid each and sell them for six or seven. That's a big profit for you – although I'll need a decision very soon, oh yeah and payment in cash. Up front. Right away.'

James promised to think it over and asked Andy to call in again the next day. Andy had seemed a bit vague as to exactly where he had got the leads from, but the offer sounded tempting; perhaps it would help him solve his business' problems.

Table 1

James' tally sheet	
Month	Number of people entering the shop (per month)
May 2002	690
June	725
July	761
August	799
September	839
October	881
November	793
December	714
January	571
February	457
March	366
April 2003 (so far)	107

Appendix 1

> Shares on the Stock Market fell sharply yesterday after several leading economists warned of the possibility of a slowdown in economic activity. Some economic indicators point to a fall in consumer confidence over the medium term.
>
> A government spokesperson was however quite upbeat. 'The data is not conclusive,' she said. 'Some sectors of the economy are undoubtedly having a bit of difficulty but others are booming. It all depends on what you are selling.'

1 James established his business as a sole trader.

State **two** features of a sole trader. [2]

2 Outline **two** factors likely to affect James' ability to supply products to his customers. [4]

3 James opened his business in 2002 and he hoped to 'make sufficient money to retire in about 20 years time' (lines 10–11).

Analyse why James' business objectives might change over this period of time. [9]

4 Evaluate the possible ways in which James might judge the success of his first year's trading. [14]

5 Discuss whether James should buy the electric guitar leads from Andy. [14]

[OCR, June 2003]

In addition to the 43 marks on the paper there are a further 2 marks for quality of written communication.

AS Mock Exam 2

Centre number
Candidate number
Surname and initials

Business Studies

Time: 1 hour 15 minutes   Maximum marks: 60

HRM and Operations Management

Answer **both** questions

Grading
Boundary for A grade   48/60
Boundary for C grade   36/60

---

1 Study the information and answer **all** parts of the question that follows.

IS THERE ANYBODY OUT THERE?

As levels of unemployment in the UK fall, firms in some parts of the country are finding it increasingly difficult to recruit the right staff and retain them. In parts of the South East less than 2% of the working-age population is looking for a job. That is good news for anyone coming into the job market in Britain's boom areas; but it is a headache for employers, who have to offer higher salaries and find other ways of recruiting and keeping staff.

Newbury has particularly low unemployment – recently there were only 349 unfilled jobs at the Job Centre, many in retail, warehousing and transport, management and ICT.

At Regency Training Ltd, a Newbury-based company specialising in training senior managers and professionals in ICT skills, Managing Director Janice Brown says: 'We've had little response to some vacancies for trainers and administrative staff. This is a labour intensive business, and we demand high levels of skill from our trainers, who often deal with senior managers of large companies. We have a policy of internal recruitment where possible, but we have had to recruit more people externally recently.'

As well as difficulties in recruiting staff, the company struggles to retain them. Many employees only stay for a short period of time because they feel they can get a better job elsewhere. One way to reduce labour turnover, Janice Brown believes, is to provide continuous training as well as a reasonable salary. 'We believe staff will be less likely to leave if the company invests in their development.'

In addition to training, she is trying different ways to encourage employees to stay at the company such as improved benefits, better working conditions and increased responsibility. 'We have a flat organisational structure to encourage empowerment and team working. Staff are eligible for performance-related pay, a private pension and private healthcare insurance after they've been with the company for a year. Working parents are encouraged to apply for a job at the company with the option to negotiate flexible hours individually.' The working environment is also important according to Brown: 'The company provides a tennis court, gym, and a restaurant with outside garden. One of our objectives is to be seen as one of the best employers in the area.'

(a) What is meant by the following terms:

  (i) 'labour intensive' (line 10); [2]

  (ii) 'performance-related pay' (line 22)? [2]

(b) Explain **two** possible reasons why Regency Training might have preferred a policy of internal recruitment. [6]

(c) Analyse the possible **disadvantages** to a company, such as Regency Training, of using financial incentives to improve motivation. [9]

(d) Regency Training has recently had difficulty recruiting and keeping skilled workers. To what extent might effective workforce planning overcome these recruitment and retention problems? [11]

2 Study the information and answer **all** parts of the question that follows.

TO BAG A BARGAIN, THE PLACE TO BE IS SAFEWAY

What difference does a change in Chief Executive make? Plenty, judging by the recent performance of Safeway, the supermarket group. Carlos Criado-Perez joined in August 1999 and after just one year under his leadership the company has gone from strength to strength. In the 6 months to October 2000, sales rose by 5% and profits by 10%, and Safeway claims to have attracted one million new customers.

Criado-Perez came from a large US retailer and his experience told him that a long-term policy of low prices, as pursued by most of the UK supermarkets, would not work for a relatively small retailer like Safeway, which did not enjoy the same economies of scale, as the average size of its outlets was less than its rivals. Instead he decided to use a strategy of loss leading – cutting the price of 20 or so different items each week. The radical part of this strategy is that the price cuts vary from town to town and change each week. In this way Safeway can respond flexibly to changing trading conditions in different areas of the country.

But this is a high-risk strategy. Not only do sales have to increase to compensate for the price cuts, Safeway also has to get its stock control right. Controlling stock levels for different products across all the outlets in the country is extremely difficult, and Safeway has made mistakes, causing customer dissatisfaction when shelves have been left empty.

One year on from the start of the promotional campaign, Safeway remains committed to a process of continuous improvement. Through a programme of benchmarking against its rivals, Safeway constantly looks for a competitive edge. Criado-Perez is convinced that the company will succeed by adding value to the Safeway brand, through better quality products and processes, closer links with suppliers, improvements in store layout and increases in productivity.

Source: adapted from the *Observer*, 26 November 2000

(a) What is meant by the following terms:

    (i) 'benchmarking' (line 18); [2]

    (ii) 'productivity' (line 22)? [2]

(b) Explain **two** possible economies of scale that Safeway's larger rivals might have enjoyed that would allow them to pursue a permanent low-price policy. [6]

(c) Safeway's promotional strategy is to cut the prices of a constantly changing selection of products. Examine the possible stock control problems that Safeway might have experienced as a result of this policy. [9]

(d) To what extent might the success of Safeway's process of continuous improvement be dependent on the quality of its staff? [11]

[AQA, January 2002]

AS Mock Exam 3

Centre number
Candidate number
Surname and initials

Letts

Business Studies

Time: 1 hour 15 minutes   Maximum marks: 60

Accounting & Finance and Marketing

Answer **both** questions

Grading
Boundary for A grade   45/60
Boundary for C grade   30/60

---

1 Study the information and answer **all** parts of the question that follows.

Cafédirect Ltd

Cafédirect Ltd is committed to supplying consumers with good quality coffee without exploiting coffee growers in less developed countries. This is known as 'fair trade'. The company prides itself in:

- paying a fair price – often 10% above that paid by other companies
- paying growers 60% of the price when placing an order, rather than waiting until the goods are delivered.

Cafédirect admits that it is aiming to make consumers in wealthy countries, such as the UK, think about what they put in their supermarket trolleys. The company is determined to avoid forcing farmers in less developed countries to accept low prices and low living standards.

In spite of these principles the company has had low sales because most consumers are not interested in fair trade. Cafédirect took the decision to relaunch its instant coffee brand as 5065 in spring 2002. The company's market research had revealed that drinkers of instant coffee were 'turned off' by the name and packaging of the old product. Many consumers had not heard of, or seen, the product. A Cafédirect spokesperson said: 'We want to attract younger, more mainstream customers. The instant coffee market is a mainstream, mass market'. The introduction of 5065 is a move from a niche market to a mass market for Cafédirect's instant coffee brand.

The Cafédirect name will still appear on the packaging of 5065 as will a description of how fair trade helps producers. This will differentiate the product from other instant coffees. However, the packaging has been redesigned to emphasise the quality of the product. Cafédirect faces tough competition from well-known coffee producers such as Nescafé who have much more experience of selling instant coffee in a mass market.

Cafédirect received a boost to its plans to launch 5065 when the Co-op announced that it is to sell fair trade products in 1500 of its supermarkets throughout the country. The Co-op has produced leaflets and posters explaining how fair trade helps farmers in less developed countries. Cafédirect plans to promote 5065 widely. Business analysts believe that effective distribution will be vital if 5065 is to be successful in a mass market.

Source: Adapted from *MediaGuardian.co.uk* 2 January, 2002

(a) Explain what is meant by the term 'niche market' (line 15). [3]

(b) Cafédirect pays growers 60% of the price of the coffee when placing an order. Outline **one** financial benefit to coffee growers that may result from this action. [3]

(c) Cafédirect's decision to launch 5065 was based on the results of primary market research. Explain **two** reasons why the company may have decided to carry out this research. [6]

(d) Analyse **two** ways in which effective distribution might help Cafédirect to market 5065 successfully. [8]

(e) Cafédirect has decided to stop selling its instant coffee in a niche market and to launch it into a mass market. Discuss the case for and against this decision. [10]

2 Study the information and answer **all** parts of the question that follows.

Archerman plc

Archerman plc is one of the UK's largest manufacturers of electronic products. The company is well known for manufacturing a range of high quality software and components used in audio visual equipment. Despite this reputation Archerman has suffered from falling levels of profits over the last few years and has lost market share to foreign competitors. A new management team was recently appointed with the objective of improving the company's financial performance.

One of the first decisions taken by the new management team was to increase the company's production of compact disks (CDs) and digital versatile disks (DVDs). To enable this to happen Archerman intends to open a factory at Swansea in South Wales. This will allow the company to manufacture larger quantities of CDs and DVDs using the most up-to-date equipment. As a consequence Archerman expects to reduce costs and become more price competitive.

Output of CDs and DVDs per annum (millions)	Total cost of production (£ millions)
0	4.0
5	7.4
10	10.3
15	13.0
20	15.6
25	18.4

The new factory is expected to cost £20 million to build and equip and to have fixed costs of £4 million in its first year of trading. Owing to the company's low profits over recent years, external sources will be used to raise most of the capital required. The company's expected total costs for its new factory are set out above.

The company is concerned to make sure that the factory is profitable. To achieve this some managers have suggested that cost-plus pricing is used, whilst others believe they must match the prices charged by Archerman's competitors. Due to the fall in profits suffered by the company in recent years, the management team is anxious that the new factory earns profits as soon as possible. They agreed that operating the factory as a profit centre would help to achieve this aim.

(a) What is meant by the term 'profit centre' (line 20)? [2]

(b) Explain **one** disadvantage to Archerman of using cost-plus pricing for the CDs and DVDs produced at the new factory in Swansea. [4]

(c) Archerman plc has set a price of £1.10 per disk.

   (i) Calculate the level of profit or loss the company will earn from the new factory if it produces and sells 5 million disks per year. [3]

   (ii) Calculate the contribution received per disk if the factory produces and sells 15 million disks per year. [4]

(d) Archerman plc needs to raise £20 million to build and equip its new factory in Swansea. Analyse **two external** sources of finance Archerman might use to raise the funds it requires. [8]

(e) To what extent is it vital for the Swansea factory to earn profits in the short-run in these circumstances? [9]

[AQA, January 2003]

AS Mock Exam Answers

PAPER 1

(1) The two features could come from the following list:

- Unlimited liability
- The owner keeps all the profit
- The owner has to cover all the losses
- Limited amount of capital available
- The owner makes all the decisions
- Only one source of ideas/expertise

1 mark for each feature stated

> **examiner's tip** If a question asks you to state something then you do not need to go into any depth to explain. A statement of fact is all that is required. Keep your answer very brief.

(2) Factors that affect James' ability to supply include:

- High costs of stock will mean that with a limited budget James will be able to hold less stock in the shop.
- Higher prices may encourage James to supply more in anticipation of greater profits.
- Increased VAT would reduce James' willingness to supply, as an indirect tax increase is equivalent to a rise in costs.
- The lack of local competition (line 5) will mean that James will expect to supply more.
- The length of the shop's opening hours will clearly affect the potential to supply.

1–2 marks – Up to two factors listed
3–4 marks – Up to two factors explained

> **examiner's tip** Do not confuse demand and supply. If a question asks about supply factors then be careful not to talk about demand at all.

(3) Initially James' objectives will have been survival and getting known in the local community. Once he was established then he would be able to build on this. In the medium term James would begin to consider objectives such as profit and growth. In the long run, if James is going to retire from the proceeds in 20 years time, he must achieve a certain amount of profit.

The business environment is dynamic and so any firm will need to review and revise its objectives in the light of any changed influences, such as the emergence of a competitor or changes in costs. In particular, the evidence contained in Appendix 1 about a possible slowdown in the economy may change James' objectives in the immediate term. As music products and accessories cannot be classed as necessities, any downturn in the business cycle will lead to a fall in demand. Therefore, James must accept that his profits will fall during this period.

1–3 marks – Knowledge of objectives and/or why they might change
4–7 marks – Understanding of reasons for changes in objectives for James' business
8–9 marks – Analysis of the reasons why James' objectives will need to change

(4) Success can be measured in many ways:
- Many new businesses fail in their first year and so survival could be considered as evidence of success for James.
- Is the fact that James' business has not grown as fast as he hoped a sign of failure? Surely he was far too optimistic.
- James is said to be concerned about his ability to pay interest on his loans (line 36). Is this a sign of a lack of success or just to be expected of a small business just starting up?
- The fact that James is running his own business and is his own boss could be a measure of success. Is he happier than before? Does he have sufficient leisure time?
- Table 1 provides some evidence that James himself has collected to measure his 'success'. It shows a 5% rise in visits until the end of October, but a 10% fall in November and December and 20% afterwards. Is this a sign of success or otherwise?
    - However, James has only recorded visitors to the shop – it does not mean that they actually bought anything. Initially the high visitor numbers may have been because of people coming 'to have a look' but not buying. Some of these may have returned later on and bought something.
    - How accurate are James' figures? We are told that James only kept these figures 'when he remembered' (line 21).
    - A better measure that James could keep is the value or volume of sales.

    1–3 marks   – Knowledge of possible methods to judge success
    4–6 marks   – Understanding of the methods that could be used
    7–10 marks – Methods analysed in the context of Jam at James
    11–14 marks – Evaluation of possible methods that James might use – in particular, the usefulness of Table 1

(5) The main issues to be considered when discussing whether James should buy the electric guitar leads from Andy are legal and ethical.
- The Sale of Goods Act states that goods must be 'of satisfactory quality' and 'fit for their purpose'. If James tries to sell the leads as if they were 'normal quality' this could be deemed to be illegal. If he chooses to sell them as 'seconds' this may not be the case, but would it be unethical given that James knows how poor the quality actually is?
- Andy is very vague as to the exact origin of the leads – it sounds as though they 'fell off the back of a lorry'! In which case, James could face criminal charges for 'receiving' stolen goods and his reputation could be affected by the bad publicity that he would receive.
- If the leads are in fact legitimate they could provide James with some 'easy money'. But how long will it take him to sell them, especially if there is a recession looming? Would he 'upset' his current supplier? Has James got the necessary cash 'up front'?

    1–3 marks   – Knowledge about legal and/or ethical issues
    4–6 marks   – Understanding shown about the legal & ethical issues facing James
    7–10 marks – Analysis of the decision that James faces and discussion of any possible impact on his business
    11–14 marks – A supported decision about whether James should or should not buy the leads. This may depend on James' conscience, how he chooses to market the leads and his objectives

> **examiner's tip** Wherever possible, always try to make a decision when faced with a question such as this. As long as your decision is supported then it is a relatively easy way to show evaluation and so gain top marks.

AS Mock Exam Answers

PAPER 2

(1) (a) (i) A process which relies on workers rather than machinery. Labour costs will represent a large proportion of total costs. **(2)**

(ii) A scheme that links annual salary to an employee's performance in the job. **(2)**

(b) Reasons for internal recruitment include:
- Existing employees are familiar with the company so Regency would not have to spend as much time and money on induction.
- Regency would have had better knowledge of the candidates and been able to make an informed choice amongst applications.
- Regency's employees might have seen promotional prospects as a reason to stay with the company.

0–2 marks – Up to two reasons listed, but with no link to Regency
3–6 marks – Up to two reasons explained in relation to Regency

(c) Possible disadvantages of financial incentives include:
- Most motivational theorists do not support the idea that money is a successful motivator.
- It is not always possible to link effort with reward – this is particularly true for Regency Training. How can you measure the 'output' of a training company?
- Is financial motivation rewarding quantity rather than quality of output? Again, Regency's work is very quality based.
- The level of output for Regency Training will be greatly affected by external factors, such as the state of the economy. In a recession, this sort of business demand will fall significantly. Therefore, the performance-related pay of Regency's employees will be partly out of their hands.
- Regency are emphasising the importance of team working. Financial motivators are very divisive. How is the work of individual team members assessed?

0–2 marks – Two or more disadvantages stated
3–5 marks – Disadvantages explained that are relevant to Regency
6–9 marks – Disadvantages analysed in the context of Regency

(d) Effective workforce planning will help with:
- Forecasts of labour demand can be matched by labour supply – recruitment drives can anticipate increases in demand.
- Anticipating short-term labour shortages and identifying long-term labour needs. Recruitment can then match these needs.
- Analysing the current labour force to identify any skills gaps. We are told that Regency Training has taken steps to encourage working parents back to work with flexible hours.

However, workforce planning may not prevent:
- Skill shortages that are a regional or national phenomenon.
- External factors, such as the cost of living in the area and competition levels, influencing recruitment difficulties. For example, Newbury is a very expensive place to live.

0–2 marks – Knowledge of what workforce planning is
3–8 marks – Analysis of how workforce planning will impact on recruitment and/or retention of staff of Regency Training
9–11 marks – Evaluation that attempts to balance the benefits of planning with recognition that no business can completely isolate itself from the impact of such situations. Ultimately, planning **reduces** rather than removes uncertainty

(2) (a) (i) The establishment of targets based on the performance of leading competitors. (2)

(ii) A measure of the output per unit of input. Most likely to be output or sales per worker over a period of time. (2)

(b) Economies of scale enjoyed by Safeway's rivals include:
- Purchasing & Marketing economies – better rates when purchasing products from suppliers, especially considering Safeway's localised promotion. Also, a national advertising campaign would be more cost effective than Safeway's localised policy.
- Technical economies – the benefits of increased dimensions could be applied to retail outlets. This explains the much bigger Tesco and Sainsbury's stores.

0–2 marks – Two or more economies of scale stated
3–6 marks – Economies of scale explained in relation to rival stores' low-price policy

(c) Possible stock control problems include:
- Costs of stock out – Safeway's local reputation will be damaged if shelves are empty of the low-price goods for that particular store.
- Storage costs of the promoted items – those products being promoted at that moment in a particular store will require a larger buffer stock. These costs will not be offset by the lower ordering costs expected if stocks were permanently high.
- Problems of negotiating shorter lead times of the current low-price products. As these products will be constantly changing and each store is different, a huge amount of planning (in terms of time and financial costs) will be necessary.
- Opportunity costs of too much stock. Stock levels will depend on accurate market information, which again will be more difficult because of the localised nature of Safeway's policy.

0–2 marks – Two or more stock control problems identified
3–5 marks – Application of stock control problems to Safeway's situation
6–9 marks – Analysis of the stock control problems created for Safeway of their promotional policy, using effective theory

(d) Possible answers include:
- Supermarkets measure quality based on satisfying customer needs. Staff are best placed to identify this, especially at local level.
- The success of continuous improvement (Kaizen) is dependent on staff involvement.
- Retailing is predominantly a labour-intensive activity. Therefore Safeway's success will be based heavily on the quality of their staff.
- Continuous improvement leads to change, which can lead to resistance, particularly if linked with productivity. Therefore, the co-operation of staff is vital for the success of such a scheme.
- The high level of price competitiveness in the UK retail sector may mean that success is wholly dependent on a low-price policy, regardless of other factors such as the quality of staff.

0–2 marks – Knowledge about quality or continuous improvement, unrelated to Safeway's activities
3–8 marks – Analysis, linked to Safeway, of the importance of quality of staff to continuous improvement
9–11 marks – Evaluation that attempts to judge the significance of the human resource in a labour-intensive business

AS Mock Exam Answers

PAPER 3

(1) (a) A niche market is a targeted small segment within a larger market. (3)

(b) It will increase their cash income – which is likely to be important to coffee growers who have a limited cash inflow, for example in helping them avoid borrowing and therefore interest costs.

0–1 marks – Knowledge of cash flow is shown
2–3 marks – Linking to the context of coffee growers

> **examiner's tip** 'Outline' requires you to explain the point you have made in context.

(c) Reasons why the company may have decided to carry out primary research include:
- Cafédirect may have wanted to discover how its potential consumers are likely to react to its 'fair trade' unique selling point.
- The context does not indicate that Cafédirect has a lot of experience of selling instant coffee in a mass market, and so it needed to find out more about its consumers and market.
- Cafédirect may be faced with the situation of poor sales for its products; as a result, it would need additional market information before being able to develop a new marketing strategy.

0–2 marks – Up to two relevant reasons for primary research
3–6 marks – Up to two reasons fully explained in relation to Cafédirect

(d) Two ways in which effective distribution might help Cafédirect to market 5065 successfully include:
- Instant coffee may be price-sensitive, so it is necessary to control costs: efficient distribution will help Cafédirect achieve this aim by making its product price-competitive.
- Cafédirect's marketing strategy is now based on mass marketing, and therefore the company must ensure that 5065 instant coffee is available in a large number of outlets: efficient distribution will help the company achieve this.
- Cafédirect will want to establish brand loyalty, and therefore the product must be widely and regularly available: efficient distribution is therefore necessary.
- Some consumers may buy on impulse: without efficient distribution, the 5065 instant coffee will not be available to take advantage of this feature.

0–2 mark – Up to two relevant ways distribution is important
3–4 marks – Effective application of distribution to the context
5–8 marks – Implications of effective distribution analysed in context

> **examiner's tip** You can present a one-sided answer here because you are asked to 'Analyse' ways to market 'successfully'. There is no need to present a conclusion.

(e) Arguments for this decision include:
- The context indicates that Cafédirect's old product was not selling well, and therefore the company needed to take action to remedy this problem.
- Market research mentioned in the context suggests that selling instant coffee to a mass market is more appropriate than selling it to a niche market.
- Cafédirect has the backing of at least one national retailer (the Co-op), which will support its aim to sell in the mass market.
- Cafédirect can differentiate the 5065 instant coffee through its 'fair trade' context, which will help in promoting and selling this product.

Arguments against this decision include:
- Cafédirect appears to have little knowledge of the consumers who buy mass-marketed instant coffee.
- There is some evidence that these consumers are not heavily interested in 'fair trade' products, and therefore Cafédirect's USP may be of limited value only.
- If price is the main determinant of buying coffee in the mass market, Cafédirect may not be price-competitive as a result of its 'fair trade' policy.
- So far, Cafédirect only has the support of the Co-op, and will need to sell through at least some other major national retail outlets such as Tesco and Sainsbury.

0–2 marks – Knowledge of the main markets and market factors
3–7 marks – Suitable application to the context of selling instant coffee in a mass market, and good analysis of Cafédirect's situation
8–10 marks – Evaluation that attempts to balance the 'for' and 'against' arguments associated with Cafédirect's decision to move into the mass market.

examiner's tip — This part of the question is at Evaluation level, so you therefore need to present a conclusion that is balanced.

(2) (a) A profit centre is a part of a business – for example, one of its departments or product lines – against which costs and revenues can be located. As a result, profit can be calculated for this centre/location.

(b) Disadvantages to Archerman plc from using cost-plus pricing in this context include:
- There is evidence in the context that Archerman plc faces competition, which is likely to be on price. Cost-plus pricing ignores prices of competitors, and may therefore not give Archerman plc the information it needs.
- Cost-plus pricing, to help most effectively in decision-making, relies on all output being sold, and there is no indication that Archerman plc will be able to do this, since evidence shows that it is increasing substantially its output.

0–2 marks – Knowledge of cost-plus pricing is shown
3–4 marks – One disadvantage is identified and related in context to Archerman plc

(c) (i) Sales revenue = £1.10 × 5 000 000 = £5 500 000
Costs (shown in the table) = £7 400 000
Overall loss = £7 400 000 – £5 500 000 = £1 900 000

0–1 mark – Some knowledge of profit/loss, costs and revenues
2–3 marks – Calculation of loss

(ii) Revenue per disk = £1.10
Total costs at 15 million output are £13m
Variable costs at this output are £9m
(calculated £13m – £4m [at zero output])
Unit variable cost (£9m/15m) = £0.60
Unit contribution (revenue – variable cost) = £0.50

0–1 mark – Some understanding of contribution
2–4 marks – Calculation of contribution

examiner's tip — Always check the figures given at zero output, to discover the fixed costs.

(d) Two external sources of finance Archerman plc might use to raise these funds include:

- A loan from a bank. The bank is unlikely to provide the full £20 million, and may not consider lending to a company with a recent record of low profits. Archerman plc will face interest costs.
- More share capital issued. Archerman plc will avoid interest costs but will face costs of issuing, and there will be an expectation that dividends will be paid (out of taxed profit, unlike interest which is paid out of untaxed profit). Archerman plc's recent profits record may make it difficult to sell the new shares.
- Debenture issue. Again, Archerman plc will face interest costs and will have to redeem the loan at some stage. There is likely to be a fixed rate of interest, which may make it attractive to Archerman plc.
- Venture capital. As a plc, this company may be able to attract venture capitalists willing to take a risk. However, it is unlikely that Archerman plc could raise the full £20 million from this source.
- Given the size of the amount needed, it is likely that Archerman plc will use more than one source for the funds.

0–2 marks – Some understanding of sources of finance
3–4 marks – Application to Archerman plc's situation, e.g. by referring to the size of the loan and to its recent profits record
5–8 marks – Good analysis of two external sources of finance, referring to their nature and relevance in this context

examiner's tip Note the question focuses on 'external' sources, so do not fall into the trap of including internal sources in your answer.

(e) The importance of short-term profits in these circumstances includes:

- Shareholders are more likely to be concerned about short-term profits than customers and staff.
- In the short term, cash may be more important to Archerman plc than profits, for example in terms of survival through having sufficient liquidity.
- Profits are important to Archerman plc to ensure its creditors do not lose faith in the company's ability to meet financial obligations such as repaying interest and loans.
- Given the apparent size of Archerman plc, the company can probably survive comfortably in the short term without making profits.
- The company may have to accept no short-term profits due to the time it will take for the factory to be built and to produce, and also the company to sell, the products.

0–2 marks – Some understanding of profits and other financial factors
3–6 marks – Application to Archerman plc, e.g. by reference to factory and products, and good analysis of the situation
7–9 marks – Evaluation through reaching an appropriate conclusion, and/or making suitable judgements about the likelihood and importance of profits to this company

examiner's tip There is no necessarily correct answer – you need to evaluate the position in both the short and long term.